LEONEANTHOLOGY

Contemporary Short Stories & Poems from Sierra Leone

Edited by
Gbanabom Hallowell

Leoneanthology
Contemporary Stories & Poems from Sierra Leone
Copyright © 2016 by Gbanabom Hallowell (ed.)
All rights reserved.

ISBN: 978-99910-54-22-3

Sierra Leonean Writers Series

CONTENTS

Acknowledgements

Introduction

SHORT STORIES	*SHORT STORIES*
Talabi Aisie Lucan	The First Crowing of the Cocks
Oumar Farouk Sesay	Closure
Mohamed Gibril Sesay	River Blindness
Josephine Ansumana	"Kpiangbe"
Siaka Kroma	A Man Called Scorpion
Moses Kainwo	The Thief
Gbanabom Hallowell	Virtual Intention
Arthur E.E. Smith	Mr. Democraticus Britanny Jones' Hard Day at Home
Karamoh Kabba	The Ring
Kosonike Koso-Thomas	The Pineapple Line
Prince Kenny	The Grand Reunion

POEMS

POEMS

Delphine King

Along the Marina
The Mystery of Man
The Voice of Africa

Agyeman Taqi

Corruption
Oh Sweet Salone

Elizabeth L.A. Kamara

The Harmattan
Thunderstorm in Freetown
Fourteen Athletes Missing

Oumar Farouk Sesay

I Listen
The Old Man on the Road
to Regent
A Cry for Maddie
Tears

Isa Blyden

The Wailing Winds
Ro-Marong
Kasseh…The Bai's Account

P.M. Wilson

The Lost Love
Lonely Nights Spare
Me No More

Josephine Ansumana

Holidays
The Vendor's Flight
The Immutable Power
of Foreign Aid

Moses Kainwo	A Letter to Corporal Foday Sankoh
	The Culture of Peeping
	Lebanon on the Move
Fatou Wurie	Untitled
	The Private Life of War
Richmond Smith	The Defender, my brother
	The Old Shoes
	Deep Silence
	English Language
Fatou Taqi	Woman
	The Cord
Komba David Sandi	Big Men Do Cry
	Reflections
	For Sake of Innocence
	Child Soldier
	Rebel Attack
	A Second Chance?
Mustapha Sanasie Biro	The Patriot
	War
Gbanabom Hallowell	One Night at Lumely Beach
	Bunce Island on My Mind
	Someone Had to Have Loved Madam Yoko
	The Economic Mind

	of Bai Bureh
	Gbanka of Yoni
	Kai Londo of Kailahun
	I.T.A Wallace Johnson,
	Come Forth
	King Kama Dumbuya
	A River of Two Scarcies
	Amistad of the Sierra
Mohamed Gibril Sesay	*We Marchon*
	Or Falang
	At the Gathering of the Roads
James Bernard Taylor	Dissipating Slowly
	Here Today, Gone Tomorrow
	I Refuse!
Ambrose Massaquoi	Sleepless in America
	Ibadan Revisited
	Epitaph
	Counterpoint
	Grassroots Poet
Miatta French	Offering Time
	To Sisters in High Places
	Contract for Pregnancy
	It's Never Right
	When Mama Goes
Kosonike Koso-Thomas	Fish Woman
	The Pen Road

Washer Woman

Frederick | Borbor James   The Journey
                            The Game of Chimps
                            Faint Hope
                            Ode to Tom Cauuray

                            Contributors

In memory of my father and friend,
Rev. John Ernest Hallowell
1937-2013

ACKNOWLEDGMENTS

Leoneantholgy: Contemporary Short Stories and Poems from Sierra Leone is probably the most voluminous anthology of Sierra Leonean creative writers to have been compiled. Bringing together the work of twenty-five short story writers and poets was an exciting process as well as a challenging one.

I am first of all indebted to the writers who believed in the project and submitted their works for consideration. I was apprehensive about the impossibility of 'discovering' any female Sierra Leonean writer who might want to contribute, but I was pleasantly surprised to know that as many as eight female writers were ready to contribute to this project.

I want to thank Dr. Fatou Taqi, a lecturer in the Department of Language Studies and Moses Kainwo for their editorial support, Isa Blyden, a freelance consultant, and Ivan, a Graphic Artist for designing the cover.

Funds for this project were provided by Star Communication Network Technology Co., Ltd. We thank them for this valuable contribution to the promotion of creative arts in Sierra Leone.

"War generally concentrates the mind. It forces people to reflect on their history and make them try to learn... War can galvanize people into the reflective type of literature."
                                   Eldred Durosimi Jones

INTRODUCTION

Local creative writing is still only being lethargically embraced by the wider Sierra Leonean readership. Who will blame a people for this kind of response in a country where basic needs have still not been adequately addressed; a country which has lost the passion and culture of reading, where there is no decent bookshop and where the young place emphasis on material acquisition but no value on literary works. However, with regards to bread and butter issues or basic survival needs, it has been argued that such inadequacies should motivate a people to seek avenues to express, albeit creatively, even wittily, these conditions. These avenues will not only illustrate the causes but will manifest in their own thinking, what solutions to proffer. For the same reason, a people starved of basic needs must be eager to want to see how their conditions are told in prose and poetry

It is acknowledged that creative writing, anywhere, remains a rather intensely personal affair, without being private. And indeed, it is because of the lack of privacy in creative writing that a nation should encourage the growth of its literary tradition. Writers do not just tell their stories or poets show their emotions; in their 'moods', they assume a multidimensional posture so as to be able to tell universally acceptable stories to appeal to different human senses. I say senses because creative writing is all about the ability to touch subtle nerves in the reader through the adrenaline of narratives and sensations of literary conductions. However, unless the writer's nerves are themselves first genuinely tickled, no piece by that creator will excite others.

Every writer is a product of a unique environment, a custom and a way of thinking. As well as being national, these elements can be personal. Two writers born in the same culture, environment and way of life can still have these foundations appeal differently to them as they engage in recreating an experience. These unique fundamental elements help shape the narratives of the writer, to, in turn, make his or her own writing contextually appealing to any audience.

A master storyteller, Virginia Hamilton can be appropriated as to why writers write:

> There is an important reason why I write. Telling stories allows me to connect with the past generations of my cultural group while writing about the present. I connect my writing with the future by inference of both past and present. In order to do that, I use knowledge of history and present events as well as my own experience[1]

After fifty years of independence, and even before colonial rule, there have been multidimensional narratives that the Sierra Leonean writer is blessed with to share with the world.

---

[1] Hamilton, V. (2010). "A Storyteller's Story," in *Speeches, Essays and Conversations*, Ed. Arnold Adoff & Kacy Cook, The Blue Sky Press: New York, p.244

Over the years, readers will agree that much of African narrative has been conveyed through the two major spheres of religion and politics. The potential is, however beginning to emerge for African narratives to be redirected through other metaphors such as fantasy and science. At least one story in this anthology goes in the way of fantasy, science or both.

The enchorial Sierra Leonean writer has made several attempts to own a voice on the continent. Most of these attempts, from the colonial period to present have been frustrated, not only by political interference, but by the Sierra Leonean demeanor of conformism. This condition was upheld, lingeringly, for most of our nation's fifty years since colonialism ended.

Western education came to Africa like a Trojan horse. We were so amazed by the imported knowledge from the West that we thought of knowledge as being the absolute truth in a Kantian sense. We saw ourselves as consumers of final products, products that were manufactured in the West and brought to us in giant cargo ships. The West came to us in the guise of pre-Socratic Greek philosophers like Parmenide whose "poem depicted the philosopher as an initiate who has received insight into the truth from a goddess who holds the keys of justice in her hands, Empedocles who "claimed special knowledge on the basis of his own long cycle of incarnations as 'a boy, a girl, a bush, a bird, and a dumb sea fish;'" Heraclitus who "compared his pithy aphorisms to the sayings of the Delphic oracle, implying that they contained a hidden wisdom that the listener must work to extract;" and also, like Pythagoras whose followers thought of him "as a wonder-working sage, and formed communities bound by vows of silence to perpetuate his wisdom.[2]"

It is however encouraging to note that, in Sierra Leone, a positive shift from conformism to creativism has manifested itself since the 1991-2001 civil war. In light of the increasing narratives, perhaps more than at any other time, it lies in the destiny of the contemporary Sierra Leonean writer to capture the pictures of shame and the pictures of gain.

Let us appropriate storytelling and poetry as they are generally perceived on the African continent. Storytelling is the process of unfolding strands through a series of connected and orchestrated events. In storytelling, the past becomes a fountain from which parties tap. Storytelling is a banking process in which the parties have invested, and since the art of narration is itself a healing process, parties help each other to see all perspectives of their relationships.

Contrary to what many believe, there has never been a watershed event that gave rise to a new kind of poetry in Africa even with the violent interruptions of slavery, colonialism, and imperialism. The oral is the root of the written. But given the spoils of slavery, the scramble and colonization of Africa, which also saw the plundering of early African civilization, much of our literature with no European value suffered the same sort of scorn from colonists that the African Traditional Religion did in the hands of Arab and Christian missionaries. From what we read of pre-colonial poetry handed over mostly in the oral and later transcribed, like the popular epic of *Sundiata*, one can only say that what we call a new kind of poetry is the

---

[2] Nussbaum, M. (1997). *Cultivating Humanity: A Classical Defense of Reform in Liberal Education*, Harvard University Press: Cambridge, p.20

mind of the new poet under a new hostile condition. Of this experience, the Somalian exiled writer, Nurudin Farah is quoted as saying, "I was born in the oral tradition . . . the move from oral tradition to a written tradition is itself one form of exile.[3]"

In response to an interview conducted by Elizabeth Kamara, a poet in her own right, and a contributor to this anthology, the eminent Sierra Leonean Shakespearean and Africanist scholar, Eldred Durosimi Jones noted that:

> There are all the signs that Sierra Leonean writing has a very good future. One impediment however is the lack of local publishing facilities as it is not easy for new writers to catch the attention of overseas publishers. What is badly needed is local access to publication in order to encourage the spread of the tradition of writing, out of which the international stars would emerge.[4]

The contributors to this anthology are mostly first time writers, whose works have not found access in mainstream literary journals and publications. While a few names among these contributors may be known, in the local Sierra Leonean literary circles as having produced one kind of work

---

[3] Farah, N. (1990). "In Praise of Exile" in *Literature in Exile* edited by John Glad, Duke University Press Books
[4] Jones, E. D. (2013). "An Intellectual Compass: An Interview with Elizabeth Kamara" in *Research in Sierra Leone Studies (RISLS): Weave* Vol. 1 No. 1.

or the other, their names do not usually ring a bell outside of Sierra Leone. This situation has to change and this is the reason that *Leoneanthology: Contemporary Short Stories & Poems* has been compiled and published through Sierrarts Publishing, a local publishing house.

Gbanabom Hallowell, PhD   Freetown, Sierra Leone

Leoneanthology

Talabi Aisie Lucan

THE FIRST CROWING OF THE COCKS

"Don't forget," said Kailondo to his Chief Spy. "We must attack at the first crowing of the cocks. Don't forget."

Kailondo's men rushed to hear the words of their leader.

"What did he say?" They asked.

The Chief Spy passed on the order, "We must attack at the first crowing of the cocks."

The order was passed from one man to the other. Then the men went back into the bush which was their hiding-place. It was dark and soon all was quiet.

In a village not very far away, Dawa and his men were rejoicing.

They had seized the village from the people. They had just finished building a third wall around the village. Little did they know that Kailondo and his men were near-by. There was dancing and feasting until late in the night. Then Dawa went into his hut to sleep. His men went to sleep too.

Kailondo lay awake all night. His Chief Spy was also awake.

As soon as it was time, they woke the sleeping men up. Quietly, they picked up their spears and they walked along the narrow path leading to the village. When they reached near the first wall, they all stopped. The Chief Spy went forward and listened. He heard nothing. He looked around. He saw nothing. All was quiet. He hurried back and told Kailondo. Kailondo and the men moved forward. When they reached the wall, they surrounded it. They then began to climb to the top. The Chief Spy was the first to reach the top. He jumped down to the other side and quickly looked round. All was silent. He gave a faint whistle and Kailondo jumped down. The men followed. Quietly they moved on to the second wall. The Chief Spy climbed to the top and jumped down to the other side. He quickly looked round. Again all was silent. He gave a faint whistle and Kailondo and his men climbed the second wall. Then they jumped down between the last two walls. Suddenly they heard some sound on the other side of the third wall. The Chief Spy ran forward and listened. All the men stood still and listened.

The sound came from Dawa's men who were asleep outside the huts. They were snoring. Kailondo's men nearly laughed when they found out that Dawa's men were snoring. The Chief Spy moved round the wall until he came to a place where there were no sounds. He whistled faintly and Kailondo led his men to the spot. This time Kailondo climbed first, followed by his Chief Spy and the rest of his men. As soon as he jumped into the village the cocks began to crow. .

Kailondo knew that Dawa and his men would be awakened by the crowing of the cocks. So as his men jumped into the village. Kailondo shouted, "Dawa, where are you? I am Kailondo, I have jumped into your village."Ced Dawa's men attempted to attack Kailondo, but Dawa rushed out of his hut and ordered them to stop. Then he walked up to Kailondo who was standing in the middle of the village. "You have met Dawa," he said. Then for a minute they stared at each other whilst their men surrounded them. Suddenly, they attacked each other. The men were tense. They looked on as Kailondo swung his sword at Dawa and Dawa swung his sword at Kailondo. Dawa was first to strike

Kailondo with his sword on his right arm. Quickly Kailondo transferred his sword to his left hand and hit Dawa with it on his forehead. Dawa's sword dropped to the ground. Kailondo could have killed him there and then, but he did not. Instead he dropped his sword to the ground and grabbed Dawa.

The two leaders wrestled with each other. Their men spurred them on. At one moment it looked as if Kailondo would be thrown. The men spurred them on and each side cheered its own leader. Kailondo noticed that his arm was bleeding badly, so he tried hard to throw Dawa to the ground. Dawa stumbled and Kailondo shouted to his men, "I have caught him, now my men, join me." Kailondo's men rushed in and one of them struck Dawa.

Dawa's men came to his help but they were too late. Dawa was in the hands of the enemies. He shouted "Please, leave me; a warrior should not kill another warrior." Kailondo replied, "We shall leave you if you promise to go away from this village and from this chiefdom." Kailondo then ordered him to go out at once. Dawa's men were all taken as prisoners together with his wife and his sons. When the people in all the villages around heard that Kailondo had won the fight with Dawa, they were very pleased. Kailondo was born in a nearby village, but Dawa came from far away. The people all came to meet Kailondo. They rejoiced with him and made him their Chief.

Kailondo's men said, "We won because we attacked Dawa at the first crowing of the cocks."

Kailondo then called together all the Chiefs from the towns and villages around for a meeting. At this meeting the Chiefs agreed to give the whole area to Kailondo. Chief

Bondo spoke on behalf of all those present. He put some earth in a white cloth, and giving it to Kailondo, he said, "Kailondo, as you have defended us, we therefore give you this land, and we will never rebel against you." All the other chiefs joined Chief Bondo in this. They all swore that they would always be loyal to Kailondo. Then it was Kailondo's turn to speak. He said, "My brothers, thank you for the trust you have shown for me. As you trust me, I will never let you down. I will never allow this chiefdom to be conquered in war." When he had finished speaking, Kailondo swore that he would keep his promise. So Kailondo became Paramount Chief of Luawa Chiefdom.

When Dawa heard what had happened he sent a message to Kailondo begging him to send his wife and his son back to him. He promised that he would never fight against Luawa Chiefdom again. Kailondo was pleased with the message. He sent a message to Dawa that he would meet him at a village called Gujehun. Kailondo took Dawa's wife and his son to Gujehun and there he handed them over to Dawa. Dawa was so pleased that he told his musicians to go with Kailondo and to play for him always. Before they parted there was dancing and singing until late at night. Then they all rested until the first crowing of the cocks, when Kailondo and Dawa said good bye to each other.

Gbanabom Hallowell (ed.)

Oumar Farouk Sesay

CLOSURE

I could not reach the dial of my transistor radio from where I was crouching. Even if I had reached it, with the stumps the rebels had left on me in their "short and long sleeve" orgy, I couldn't change the dial. I had to contend with a distorted broadcast from two frequencies battling to dominate the air waves. I took sides, I would have loved to listen to the station playing a tune from yester-years rather than the station ranting about closure and forgiveness; but like the war that preceded this airwave war, it is hard to discern a winner.

The dial seemed to be stuck between two frequencies; as such the broadcast came in a stutter, sometimes in high pitch, at times in subdued notes. At times the broadcast from one station was more audible and the other came like a chorus of stutterers. Yet I was able to make sense of the debate on the station;

'The final verdict on those who bear the greatest responsibility for the decade old war has been given today at the United Nations backed Special Court in Sierra Leone," the voice of the speaker filled the air. After that, the other station infringed with a song from a bygone era when nothing was cracked open and no need for sensitising the public about closure; it serenaded a Sierra Leone I knew and loved as I was about to be transported to that Sierra Leone. The frequency was jammed again and the stuttering of closure from the other station intruded. "Apart from the rebel leader, Corporal Foday Sankoh, and the civil defence leader, Sam Hinga Norman, who died during the trial, eight men were convicted, given long sentences, and were to be flown today to Rwanda to serve their prison terms."

Another interlude from the music station stuttered through; the stations were indeed fighting a war of narrative. It sounded like a war between two frequencies, as to whose narrative should survive. The station with the closure debate cut in again like an incoherent disc jockey; "the major trial yet to be completed is that of the Liberian leader, Charles Taylor, in The Hague". A prolonged hissing sound before the buzz phrase I hated came: "According to the presiding judge." A closure of the bloody chapter of the nation's history has been attained. Today the nation breathes a sigh of relief" '

I sighed in anger as I heard the radio blaring about closure, with a note of finality, like a concerto of a demented composer. I kicked the radio to silence it since I could not reach it from my crouching position in the toilet or change the dial with my limbless hands.

Like the stations, I was stuck between the world I knew and the new and sordid world the rebels created for me; my emotional dial swung between modes the one with the high voltage transmitter, transmitting the wreck inside me making me a transmitter of pain of my nation's hurt. I wish I could close their station forever and stop their ranting about a closure that opened the bolted gates of my soul.

I repeated the word 'closure' several times until the bitterness it conjured within me filled my mouth like bitter kola. I started to chew it with gusto as if to wipe it from the minds of men. I chewed until it felt like slime, and I spat it on a puddle of water on the crevices ridden floor. The flies hovering over my rear side abandoned my excrement and buzzed toward the spittle of closure. It seemed the smell of spittle stung more than my excrement. I watched them devouring the spittle as I contemplated the gorge opening in my soul by this so-called closure.

I was through emptying my bowels; the first such act for the past three days since Batheh, my life love, left in search of her own closure. I have been putting off the idea of going to the toilet because I couldn't think of a way of cleaning my rear without Batheh. In fact, I was scared of life without Batheh, or better still I had no life without the woman who gave hope to me after the rebels left me with three stumps: my limbs and the one that used to dangle between my legs.

The thought of the disfigurement that made me an icon of my country's tragedy sent excruciating pain through the scrum of my heart. I recalled the day like it was a billboard of shame, hoisted on my mind, advertising the looting of my manhood. The rebels had stripped me naked and chopped my limbs; one of them said the thing between my legs was bigger than his. I must be re-circumcised to ensure equality. His idea of equality made a Louis XVI of my manhood, with a machete for a guillotine in a twisted rendition of freedom, equality and fraternity. Since then, I had been left with only a tongue to replicate one of the functions of the thing that made me a Man.

Ever since that day when my body was made a terrain for these dangerous acts of revulsion my life had become nothing but a tapestry of pain. Yet nothing had prepared me for the pain I felt when Batheh left me in search of a closure. The cadence of her anguish-laden voice lingered in my soul. I could still hear her rationalization for leaving echoing, "

Bobson, my darling, I must go in search of this boy, he is my son, despite the fact that I got him from being raped; they say half a loaf is better than none."

"But this is not a loaf, it is a person we are talking about. Let the orphanage take care of him. Bringing him here will just open a bigger gorge between us," I said.

"I can't do that anymore, I need closure; I need to move on, and I can't move on with a whole of me stuck in the past. I need to confront the past to reconcile my present."

"But, what about us, Batheh?"

"I am doing it for us; your condition won't get me a baby; it is better to have this child, that is, at least, part of us. He is only a child; he had no say in the circumstances surrounding his birth"

My mind oscillated between the words 'closure' and 'condition.' The subtext embedded in the text sneered at me hurting the remains of my dignity. The anger swelled inside me and I chewed the remains of closure in my mouth, hoping to obliterate it and the pain it was pouring in my life of anguish. I scooped my mouth with my tongue, gathering the spittle of closure and spat again on the floor.

The word has not only taken a life of its own but an opinion too. It chose to sojourn inside me, knocking down doors I had barricaded since the end of the war. The irony was that the word 'closure' opened gulfs inside my soul. As I sat on the toilet box contemplating the possible ways of cleaning my rear, my mind made a backward leap to the days when I had first met Batheh, that night we went out. The thought of it all showed like the sun after a solar eclipse.

If Batheh were here, she would have cleaned me like a baby, dressed me up and fed me. Now, in her absence, I was confronted for the first time with the dilemma of living alone, without limbs. I missed Batheh; but I couldn't tell what missed her most; my heart or the necessity of my existence.

I reflected on the first night I had with Batheh.

I had left home that day with excitement, like a school boy on a first date. As I drove to her home, the tension within me increased. The closer I got to her home, the more tense I was .My feeling for her was so strong, the fear of putting a foot wrong grabbed my whole being. What if she was not interested in me? What if she was just being nice by accepting my offer of a night out? What if I made a wrong move and she refused to see me forever?

The hypotheses were like fetters paralysing my whole being. I finally arrived at her place, and I struggled to haul myself out of the car, almost cramped by the excitement. I mustered the courage to approach the gate. I took a deep sigh and imported all the ideas of composure I had learnt in my theatre days. I almost got my adrenalin flow right, after a series of breathing exercises when a barking dog materialised, rocking my composure like a boat tossed into a furious sea. At that moment I heard her sweet voice cautioning the dog. The voice gave me hope. I held on to the hope as if it was a life jacket.

After the dog had been silenced, I was a little bit relaxed. I made some mental calculus, propped on traditional logic, and I deduced my salvation from the silencing of the dog. She had the option to have unleashed the dog on me but she didn't. I mused. Ordering the dog to accept me might be a prologue to my acceptance. My mind leaped to the dog in the story of Laila and Majenun, The envy Majenun had for the dog living in the same side of town with his Laila. I envied the dog a little because she patted her tenderly as she spoke to me. I would have loved to feel the tenderness of her palm. For a brief second I wished to trade places with the dog, just to get the love that was propelling the caressing strokes.

I am not a fool like Majenun, but I am beginning to see a parallel in our feelings towards the dog and the women of our hearts.

I unleashed my mind from the dog and hooked the leash in my soul. I felt possessed by a force beyond my comprehension. I saw her with all her might, the conquering angel of my heart. She stood in front of me in black evening dress, which accentuated her bright complexion. In the starless night and black dress she glowed like a shaft of light. Her beauty jammed my sense of sight, her perfume attacked my nostrils, her voice invaded my ears and her body chemistry paralysed my whole being. Rivulets of sweat cascaded on my face, and what seemed like a leaking pipe burst under my armpit, shaming my deodorant.

The perfume I was wearing came to the rescue but was subdued by the chemicals of my body. I stood stiff like an actor gripped by stage fright. I lost my rehearsed line. I had planned to open the door for her like they do in the movies and move round to the driving seat. I lost my cue, I lost my tongue and I lost my sense of self. She saw my dilemma and jumped into the passenger seat. Once I was behind the wheels, I went for the pedals of the car, not knowing which pedals to press or gears to shift. In all my days of frolicking with women, no single woman had had such an effect on me. I steered the car in the direction of Alexe's Beach Bar, the only place I knew would help me hold on to such a beauty.

During the five kilometre drive, I had battled to gain possession of my entire entity that I had willingly given her the moment she opened the door.

Through an act of God or cupid, we finally arrived at Alexe's after shifting several wrong gears and pressing wrong pedals. The car succumbed to the torture and got us to the restaurant. We took a seat close to the edge of the ocean. The sea waves winced like passing notes in a classic song, harmonizing gently with the soft music being whispered by the speakers. The light of the candles on the tables created silhouettes of shadows and we melted in the shadows of the night: our shadows and the night and the thoughts rummaging our souls became one. That oneness had defined our relationship since that night.

We placed our orders through a rather polite waiter. From the order she placed, I learnt Batheh was a woman with a mind of her own, who knew what she wanted. We started a rather cautious conversation, sometimes punctuated by the waiter. The dialogue shifted gears to top knot speed; it skidded and screeched on bumpy terrains of our lives. We finally arrived at that zone where the souls started to speak to each other. We both started spilling our souls like showers of rain on each other.

The stiff atmosphere, characteristic of a first date, started to melt away. She aroused me in every dimension of the word. Her acumen belied her age. In her free spirit, I saw a woman of my dream. Something bigger than me took possession of my body and soul. The desire to have her to live my life for her grabbed every inch of my human estate. It seemed as if she was placing pegs on every territory of my heart. By the time the evening wore out I was a conquered territory and she my conquistador. The moment was so heavenly I wished the world to pause so that I could hold it in my psyche forever. The rawness of our humanity and my desire for her took the better part of me.

At a glance, I saw her long slender legs underneath the table. I thought of what it would feel like to feel the touch of her bare skin and to feel the pulsating pulse of her body and to smell her humanity. I imagined her heart beating next to mine, hers the lead; mine the chorus: what a beautiful classic that would be. The unwritten script of our yet to be harmonized hearts filled my ears and I sang a song that had never been sung before that night. And my soul danced.

I drove her home and tried to act in a gentlemanly way. Batheh saw my dilemma, grabbed me by her doorstep and kissed me goodnight. On my return home I was so busy savouring the kiss I could not stay focused on the road: I plunged the car into a gutter.

That night was the start of a love affair that confirmed to me that the classic love stories in movies might just be true. The human heart is capable of loving like the protagonist in fiction. In my case, her real name was Fatima, but I gave her the name Batheh, which in my mother tongue means *the most loved and favoured one*. It was a long time ago.

The smell of the latrine and the buzzing flies brought me back to my predicament. I watched the toilet roll lying on the floor. I needed a pair of hands to use it. I looked at the bowl of water that calculated to me as if I was climbing the steep and mountainous Bintumani hill barefooted.

My eyes shifted to one of the sticks used as a pillar to build the corrugated zinc toilet. But there was a nail protruding from the angle where my rear could have adequately rested. I needed to negotiate that nail to prevent another disaster.

The radio hissed and came alive in defiance of my wished-for closure; it started to blare the inaudible news about the other *closure*. I wanted to smash it but I needed to restrain my movement to prevent the faeces from rubbing all over me.

I thought of Batheh as she had bade farewell, to go in search of the son she had left in an orphanage almost a decade ago in the name of closure. Sometimes, in my quiet moments, I would try to understand her pain of being married to a man whose arousal raged within him, but lacked the organ to express his feelings.

I recalled the many failed attempts to meet my marital duties with my mutilated genitals. She would lay naked staring at the ceilings with rivulets of tears dripping from her beautiful eyes. The decibel of the unspoken word is so loud that it echoed in every recess of my being. The guns that had been silenced for a decade would suddenly erupt within me and I found myself in the war zone, right in my bedroom. The acknowledgement she gave to me in our first intimate moment faded in the distance, drowned by the cacophony of the moment.

Batheh, had managed to stay true to the punctuated wedding vow she made to me, but the son left in the orphanage tore her apart. The talk of closure in the media offered her a solution and I am left to battle with my closure.

My eyes focused on the stick with the nail that I intended to use as a toilet roll. The technique was to let the stick wedge in the cleavage of my rear before I moved slowly down with a backward thrust, wiping my rear in the process; however, the problem was the nail. The position of the nail was right at the point of departure. I needed to do some manoeuvring to clean myself, without getting my behind on the nail. I thought of the toilet I saw in a documentary in Japan that cleans one's rear after using the toilet. I dreamt of that toilet every day. Once, I approached the chairman of the Truth and Reconciliation Commission to include that toilet as reparation package for all amputees, but my appeal fell on deaf ears. I cannot comprehend how millions of dollars could have been spent in the process of transitional justice, millions more spent to resettle the villains of the atrocities in the name of reconciliation and reintegration without anyone thinking of restoring the dignity of the amputees with a toilet that cleans their rear. My mind made a dash to Pablo Neruda's poem "The Book of Questions":

How can I heal if the violence has not ended?
But how long do I wait for violence to end before starting?
How can I heal if it is dangerous to talk about what happened to me
and my family?
In what tense do we conjugate healing from collective
Violence and massacres? Past? Present? Future?

What do we do with two hundred orphans in one set of villages?
How can we accept the very people who took the lives of
their parents back into our villages?
Will even God forgive those men with the chain saws and
laughter on their faces who took both arms of the father
in front of his children?

How do we reconcile with people we never knew?
Why did the government give money to the demobilized?
militia commander but nothing to the families he killed?
How can we reconcile with people who never
admitted doing anything wrong?
How do I prove I am a victim?

Where are the remains of my father?
When do we get to go home?
Is it safe?

Where was God?
Where is GOD?

Every line of Neruda's poem opened doors bolted deep down in the trenches of my soul. It seemed the croaking voice from the radio extolling the need for closure was competing with the lines of Neruda's poem word for word, logic for logic. Where was God? Where is God? The last line unhinged my faith and flung the closed door of my soul wide open in mockery of the United Nations Special Court induced closure.

The talk of closure, with the opening of a gulf in my soul every day, annoyed me. I looked at the radio cracking on the floor in defiance of my wish, and my mind leapt back to the day that epitomized the fate of my nation, harked like my limbs.

It was our wedding day, and the guests had assembled in the church. Batheh, in her white bridal dress, looked like a goddess; followed by the little maids dropping petals as she walked up to the altar. I was clad in a three-piece embroidery gown, made in Makeni. The well-wishers, relatives and friends were as colourful as the bride and groom. The music from the assembly of musicians filtered throughout the church, as the minister performed the wedding vows: "If any of you know of any just cause why these two may not be joined in holy matrimony, may you now declare it or hence forth hold your peace."

Then, as though we were in another world, a burst of gunfire shattered the serenity of the church, drowning us in shock. By the time the firing stopped half the church was drenched in blood, and people were either dead or dying. That was annihilation, not the objection the minister had in mind. The leader of the invading rebels, a self-styled 'bush general', snarled at the pastor to pronounce him and Batheh husband and wife. The pastor did so in a rather inaudible voice. Then the rebel kissed Batheh in my presence, as the pastor stood in stunned silence at what was happening to me.

The rebel leader grabbed my loins and screamed: "you are having a hard-on because I kiss my wife?"

"She is not your wife you, animal, and she will never be, not in a billion years" My words of rage drowned the cacophony of the gun shots. The orgy stopped and all guns were directed towards me. At that moment most people escaped. A trigger happy rebel placed his gun on my head, and was about to fire when General Mingo screamed at him, "Don't shoot! I have a better idea for men who challenge our authority."

His idea of asserting authority and ensuring equality left me limbless and limp between my legs. My Batheh, taken away to be the wife of the beast and now this talk about closure and final chapter opened up a schism in Batheh's head and she now wanted closure. Her idea of closure was to go in search of the son of the devil smuggled into her womb. Our very own Damien, but was he? My mind shifted through the rubble of emotions and disused thought to enter a fresh and new landscape. Underneath the rubbles a voice buried deep down within me when the edifice of my existence shattered spoke in stuttered interrogative: "Is he really a devil or just a child of circumstance? Has he got anything to do with the circumstances of his birth or was he just a victim himself? Is it right to estrange him because of the pain that his birth brought into our life?"

The questions drowned my being. I tried to bury them underneath the rubbles of anguish. The more debris I placed the more the questions emerged with unbridled reasoning and logic. The voice of my conscience began to sound like the voice of Batheh. The logic was like that of Batheh. The fire fuming in the furnace of my soul began to smoulder to flickering amber. The tide of forgiveness surged forth and ate the fire on the edge. The heat burning my being began to cool off. I then saw Batheh, and for all what she stood for in a new light. The joy she was able to share in the midst of agony. The beauty she exuded in the midst of ugliness left radiance in everyone.

The radio croaked the word closure in broken syllables but this time it had a new meaning to me. Like Batheh I needed to go past this hurt, I needed to navigate through this river of anguish. I needed to dislodge the bullet inside me if I was to have a closure and see the world in a prism similar to that of Batheh. Her willingness to forgive and forge ahead became my mantra.

I resolved to go in search of Batheh and our son but the obstacle of cleaning my rear with the nail-prone-stick, still posed a greater challenge. My eyes surveyed all the sticks, holding the corrugated zinc toilet for an alternative. I saw one, but it looked like it had been used before. I thought of who could have used it. I never had the dilemma of using toilet sticks for toilet rolls because Batheh was always there for me. I remembered a visit Hamid paid to me after Batheh left. He had asked to use the toilet.

He could be the one who had used that stick. He was a single limb amputee but that day he had a boil on the finger. He could have been faced with the indignity that I face every day and resolved it by using that stick.

My mind was about to reach out to Aziz another amputee whose teenage daughter took the responsibility of administering to his needs after the rebels killed his wife. I red flagged my thoughts because I could not accommodate the predicament of having a daughter playing the role of Batheh. Aziz's predicament goes beyond crossing the line of decency his case obliterated all lines. I imagine the indignity both Aziz and daughter were suffering, the thought left a nauseating feeling in my soul I had to muster all my soul strength to wrench my mind from their predicament and focus on mine.

Hamid's stick of shame stared at me like an obelisk of shame commissioned to dishonour him. The mark of his shame had dried up on the stick. His was not the proverbial footprint on the sands of time but anal print on a stick. I looked at both sticks, the one that was clean and unused but with a protruding nail and the other with Hamid's anal markings on the stick of shame. I tossed the two in my mind and I walked up to the Hamid stick to wipe my shame on his shame leaving the stick to behold both our shame.

Batheh's absence had stripped the world of its essence. It now looked stark naked in my eyes. My closure was to have her by my side and to learn to live with 'our' son. The phrase 'our' son left an insipid taste on my mind. Yet, not as nauseating as when I first heard it from Batheh. He has to be our son if this country was to reach a closure. I walked to my bedroom, thinking about closure, and conscious of the fact that the aperture on my rear was not as clean as I would have loved to have it clean. Every day it opened up to answer the call of nature, a debate on closure and forgiveness began in my mind. Every day, I walked on the contours of shame and indignity. The landscape of indignity was becoming as familiar to me as the back of my palm. Sometime, I saw myself as a living monument of my country's shame.

My love for Batheh surged forth like an angry ocean, lashing against the shores of my soul; the waves quenched the fire of rage inside me. I began to feel newness within. I felt ready to write the epilogue of the national tragedy my body epitomized.

I needed Batheh to inspire me with the beauty of her body and soul. I needed to dip my pen on her well to write. I needed the radiance of her soul to see the new world.

I walked past the radio stuttering closure to the open road in search of Batheh for my own closure.

Gbanabom Hallowell (ed.)

Mohamed Gibril Sesay

RIVER BLINDNESS

Pa Sorie, walking-stick between his legs, sits on a boulder on the shores of the River Pampana. His eyes are itching non-stop, sure sign that he is about to see some extraordinary thing, something that is really good or – God forbid – very bad. He rubs his eyes and looks again. Little dark dots hang over the River Pampana like swarms of blackflies. Or are the dark dots only in his eyes? Pa Sorie is an old man with dim eyes. But today he is convinced that it is not his eyes. The Pampana is stormy.

God! Perhaps they are drowned. 'No! God forbid!!.' Pa Sorie almost falls into the river as he shouts this. He looks over his back as if to see whether he is being watched. 'No!' he shouts again, 'God will not allow my son to be killed in this River Pampana!' Pa Sorie is very convinced that his just married son and his bride are in that boat on the River Pampana, with all the merry-making things for the night ahead, the revelry ahead, the dance, the everything. His relatives had gone to that faraway village to marry the woman for his son. Led by his own younger brother, the relatives left for the bride's village very early in the morning with a white cloth-wrapped calabash toted by a virgin.

Pa Sorie's mind runs to moments when he too had led wedding trains for relatives: the play of words during the ceremony; the march of mock-brides who were politely rejected by the wedding train, but not before they were given money for transport to go fetch the real bride; the mock-anger of fake husbands who would demand compensation for letting another man take the woman they had been providing for since childhood. The ceremony would go on, slowly, with all sorts of mock moves, laughter flowing unhurriedly through the valleys of the gathered souls.

In those days, people married from places close to their homes, the farthest might be the next village, or perhaps the next chiefdom; or perhaps from amongst people that a family had interacted with for long. Pa Sorie wonders why his son would insist on marrying that woman from that far off place, from a family they do not know, from a town that has a name they cannot properly pronounce. It is not good to have in-laws who laugh at you when you pronounce the name of their town. But the children of nowadays do not care about these things. Times have changed and the children now insist on what they want.

That son of his had even insisted on following the wedding train to the village. Tradition does not allow a groom to be where the customary wedding formalities are made. So his son's going to the village, hanging out in a friend's place whilst the formalities were arranged, was useless. But these children of nowadays, they even insist on doing useless things.

Pa Sorie rises from the boulder, moves his left palm across his upper face as if to wipe the mist off the air; he jerks his head forward and peers into the distance. The River Pampana is stormy; its shores are even now deserted by the sand-miners. These sand miners… they now heap a lot more sand on many more tipper trucks than before. More sand is needed to build houses all over the place for the teeming people streaming to seek their fortunes in the expanding iron ore mines. People come from every nation, black, white, yellow, and brown. His son works in one of the mines. They say he is a big man there because he has college papers and he is also a son of the district. People in the district are insisting that the jobs go to their sons and daughters with education, whilst the rent money and royalties go to the elders and those sons and daughters without education. The money Pa Sorie is contributing to his son's wedding comes from his share of the rent money for the land. His mind runs to the night ahead, to the musicians he has hired to thrill the celebrants, the revelry ahead, the dance, the everything. He sees well-wishers stringing smiles and dancing to the rhythms of the newly-weds' laughter. He is reminded of himself as a young man courting, running, swimming, active, agile, strong, clear-sighted. When he was a young man, the River Pampana never became this stormy; there were no little black dots hovering over it like swarms of black flies.

But now, these dots of night are everywhere. He looks on and on until his eyes, nay, his soul waters; salty omens running down the jowl of his presence. Why is his soul crying? Is it that his son's boat has capsized and all are drowned? Is it that his soul is wailing for a funeral to come; or is his soul already at the funeral, at the graveside as his son is lowered into a grave? What type of final resting place is it, a watery one or an earthy one with leaves stuck in the middle of the sepulcher as a marker? Is his son buried with his bride? Are they entwined? Or are they separated like the pregnant woman and the child she died trying to give birth to? Tradition demands that the unborn child should not be buried with the dead woman. So they called in some granny to ensure the separation, so that they could have two graves, one for a being that saw the world; one for another that never roamed the earth.

. Like his own son, pregnant with a bride, never gave birth to a wife; he died in wife-birth along the River Pampana. So husband and wife must be separated before burial. There will be no laying-out of his son's body. The body is not whole enough; the fishes in the Pampana have badly eaten the body; eyes plucked, nose severely pinched, manhood, husband-hood, eaten. So there is no laying-out for all to see the last of his son, clothed in white, cotton wool in his nostrils, white pillow below his head, sweet smelling perfumes sprinkled all over him. No, his son has none of those. He is taken hurriedly to the grave. Pa Sorie sees the Imam giving the funereal invocation, *'from dust we were raised, unto it is the return, from it again we shall be raised'*. He hears the dirges laden with the cries of the women; he sees the funeral march, he notices the coffin draped with a green cloth, black-inked with verses from the Koran; he recognizes the sad looks on faces burying a bridegroom and a bride; he looks away from the grave-diggers shoveling darkness over his son's body.

The darkness is the noose round his eyes, snapping the spine of his sight.

Sight. Pa Sorie sees himself being restrained as he tries to fall into his son's grave. The mourners and the grave-diggers hold on to him, his hands flailing like ill-attached thatches in the Harmattan wind. The mourners are aghast at this unmanly rendition of grief. Men do not flail their hands when they mourn. They cry within, quietly harmonizing their sobs to the beatings of their hearts. This sad music within serenades the mourner and calms the soul.

The Soul. But now Pa Sorie sees fog all around him. The fog hugs the Pampana like perhaps his son had hugged his bride. Or is it his eyes that the darkness is hugging, throttling, suffocating? The last time he visited the eye clinic the nurse said his eyes were itching from the wounds caused by the blackflies inhabiting the shores of the Pampana. 'Those flies are bad, they hatch darkness, they make people go blind.'

Go Blind. The nurse gave him some medicines, free of charge. She was kind, that nurse, one of those his people called *wuni*, a human, she showed concern, she laughed from deep within her guts, from deep within her womb, the place of children, that was probably why her laughter sounded like that of many happy babies. Or was it so. Pa Sorie tries to re-listen to the sounds of her laughter echoing from his memory. He turns his right ear towards the direction of the wind, as if that is where the sounds of memories are coming from. The sounds from the womb of the damsel are now laden with the determination of the woman not to bear children. 'No, I will rather give birth to sights.' she had told him. 'I take care of malnourished sights neglected by the wayside. I wash the wounds of the un-parented sights. I want to make naughty sights grow into the dignity of responsible seeing.'

Pa Sorie could not understand why this beautiful good mannered woman would decide against marriage and children. Is it that the men of now are not brave enough to get her? Or is she so strong as to be both beautiful and unmarried? To be, at the same time, both kind and unwed?

She was so good mannered, the nurse at the eye clinic; so unlike that other nurse at the maternity clinic to which Pa Sorie's pregnant daughter had gone. Pa Sorie heard over the radio that the drugs and services were now to be given free to pregnant women, lactating mothers and children under five. So he sent his pregnant daughter to the nurse at the maternity clinic. But that nurse demanded money. She was even rude in her demands. She told Pa Sorie's daughter to leave her office so that she could attend to those who were serious. Yes, only those who had money had serious needs for public services. Pa Sorie's daughter got out some money to give her. The nurse refused; she said Pa Sorie's daughter had insulted her by saying that the services were for free. She said Pa Sorie's daughter meant to say she the nurse was a thief, a thief of free healthcare drugs. Pa Sorie's daughter had to beg her before she took the money; Pa Sorie's daughter had to go down on the floor, make herself small, shorten her height, assume the character of a penitent wrong-doer, before that nurse could take her money and provide the service.

Service. That nurse was so unlike the one that gave the eye medicines to Pa Sorie. But Pa Sorie could not take the sight saving tabs. He thinks medicines to cure the eyes should be put on the eyes, and not taken through the mouth. He is adamant. Like the woman who thought that the sleeping tabs she was given were too small in size. She said tabs that were small in size were for children. So she swallowed lots of the sleeping pills. And she slept and slept and slept, a most peaceful sleep, the sleep of no return, the type of sleep so deep that no one could be woken up from it. Messages were sent to her children that their mother was now sleeping the deepest sleep of all. Some of her children were out of the country then, so they had to wait for them before the sleeping woman could be placed in a grave, that most nightly of sleeping chambers. They arranged for the body of the sleeping woman to be sent to the big city to be put on ice. Pa Sorie cringes at the thought of his body on ice. But this is a new tradition that is becoming fashionable, especially amongst families with lots of absentee-relatives. Before now, Muslim people were buried just a few hours after their death. But now there are many delays in many more funerals. The children are flying in from America, the cousins are flying in from England, the brothers are flying in from wherever, Africa, Europe, America. Relatives are everywhere now. This is the age of the scattered; the era of strange new happenings. One of the children of the sleeping pill woman even came with a headstone with some writing that was read to the mourners: *sleep on beloved, sleep on and take your rest, God be with you till we join you in your sleep.*

Sleep. As he stands on the banks of the River Pampana, Pa Sorie's mind races to the words the nurse at the eye clinic told him, 'if you don't take your tabs, you will go blind, dark spots will take over your eyes, you will only be able to see people in the dreams of your sleep.' Pa Sorie shouts, 'No, God forbid seven times seven!' He is not blind. The blackflies are on the river, and not in his eyes.'

The darkness hangs over the river like the smoke in the place they smoke fish. Pa Sorie used to visit that place, the place they smoke fish. Smoke upon smoke upon smoke, the skirts of the women smoking fish are always raised to wipe off the smoky tears off their eyes. So many men here like teary women mainly because the women raise their skirts to wipe off the tears, and the men have kicks at the sights of the exposed *bottom-bellies*. There are men who specialize in the art of consoling widows; they raise their skirts to wipe off their tears. Pa Sorie smiles the smile wrought by naughty memories. He had once, in his middle ages consoled his brother's widow like this.

The darkness still hangs over the Pampana like the place of the smoking fishes, those selfsame fishes that poked out his son's eyes; that severally pinched his nose; that ate his manhood; his husband-hood. Oh oh oh oh, his soul waters, salty memories running down a sore-soul, iodine on fresh wound, excruciating oh oh oh oh… this Pampana … this river, this…, this…, this river.

'What's wrong, Papa?'

'What! My son, you are here, safe, with your bride?'

'Yes Papa, we had a lovely crossing. As you can see, Papa, the Pampana is calm and clear.'

'The storm then,' says Pa Sorie, 'must be in my eyes, the darkness is in my eyes, the night is in my seeing, I must go take the tabs, I need to prevent this darkness from taking over my soul.'

Leoneanthology

Josephine Ansumana

Gbanabom Hallowell (ed.)

KPIANGBE

A long time ago, in the Gola rainforest of Pujehun District in Sierra Leone's southern province , there lived a little tyrant bird called *Kpiangbe*. *Kpiangbe* was unlike any other bird the inhabitants of the rainforest had ever seen. "C*law-winged,* a cross between a pheasant, a squirrel and a vulture. Kpiangbe was an enigma that defied all understanding. He had the near-physical appearance of a crest-headed pheasant, the skill to run and climb trees like a squealing squirrel and the ability to digest then regurgitate his food like a vulture.

Kpiangbe had a shrivelled body, no bigger than a two–week old "plucked" chick, with a comparatively small head attached to a short but slender neck. His small head was almost as bald as a vulture's. But unlike the vulture, *Kpiangbe* had a frizzy "unkempt" feathered-crest on the top of his head. Large eyes, the size of ringed saucers were plastered on either side of his head within flushed and puckered sockets surrounded by bright blue area patches. The lower part of *Kpiangbe*'s head sprouted out into an ugly, short and stout bill with a fleshy cere, shaped like a human nostril.

Kpiangbe was equally ungainly. He wobbled and clambered clumsily on medium sized legs, which allowed him to move fairly quickly through trees. His feet were comically shaped, with the fourth toe set at a right angle to the foot. This unique feature allowed *Kpiangbe* to run and climb tree branches with the agility of a squirrel. But unlike the squirrel, *Kpiangbe* had the added advantage of moving with relative ease forwards and backwards, thereby earning him the name and status of the "foul-mouth double-footed terror."

On the whole, *Kpiangbe* was basically poor at flying. While other birds swooped and soared with agility, then dived and spiraled down like roller coasters, *Kpiangbe*'s large but short and rounded wing—span did not allow him to fly, soar or spiral. Yet in spite of his many oddities, *Kpiangbe* had the loudest and most intimidating quarrelsome voice of any inhabitant of the Gola forest—-almost as loud as the Lyrebird.

He would spend most of his time roosting quietly. But when alarmed, he would flutter his large round wings, displaying grayish brown flightless feathers. Then he would scream a variety of aggressive obscene hoarse calls, in a loud intimidating quarrelsome and nasal voice -the kind of voice one would normally associate with an over powering forceful presence.

"*Kpiangbe, Kpiangbe, Kpiangbe, Kpiangbe.* I am coming out, coming out, coming out. *Hensinahuayena ngama aye touŋ ngolie a gbwa vavava.* About this time tomorrow, blood will flow; and there will be peeing like a spray pump," his threats would ring out. "*Kpiangbe, Kpiangbe, Kpiangbe, Kpiangbe.* I am coming out, coming out, coming out.

What *Kpiangbe* lacked in size, grace and wingspan he made up for in voice pitch. His intimidating voice dwarfed all other sounds around him. At the sound of his terrifying quarrelsome high pitched calls, animals of every shape and size would abandon whatever activity they were engaged in, and run for cover. Because of his loud aggressive tirades, the inhabitants of the rain forest conjured a myth and an "aura of monstrosity" around *Kpiangbe*.

Kpiangbe nested on a twig platform about five feet above ground level around swampy mangroves flood forest and river banks or sometimes deep within the Gola-forest. He would forage in the early hours of the morning to have his pick of berries and fruits, long before most of the "early birds" left their nest in the morning. And would later go fruit gathering just after the sun lost its vengeance. Then he would silently return to spend most of his time in his nest, roosting quietly, while regurgitating and digesting his meal of berries.

Like most idlers and bullies, *Kpiangbe* was inquisitive and quarrelsome, and thrived on intimidation. Most inhabitants of the rainforest hardly ever got a chance to meet *Kpiangbe*. Those who took the risk to fly within five meters of his nest were greeted with intimidating wing flaps and a barrage of loud nasal screams and cries. Some of his neighbors therefore only identified him by the sound of his loud terrifying and intimidating screams. And because of his verbosity the whole rainforest was terrified of *Kpiangbe*. Most animals therefore assumed he *must* be a "mighty giant-sized bird" with the ability to strike fear and terror into the hearts and minds of the other inhabitants

Occasionally, *Kpiangbe* could be espied perched along waterways just whiling away the time, or roosting on treetops surrounded by thick overhanging branches of vegetation that camouflaged his small stature. He would fiercely critique the pitch of the notes in the operatic symphony conducted by the African Shrikes, who were famous for their magnificent musical repetitive duets. He would compete with the dawn chorus of the Skylark or rudely interrupt the night chorale of the Nightingale as he advertised and flexed his muscles.

"Kpiangbe, Kpiangbe, Kpiangbe, Kpiangbe. I am coming out, coming out, coming out. Hensinahuayena ngama aye touŋ ngolie a gbwa vavava. About this time tomorrow, blood will flow; and pee will spray like a pump. *Kpiangbe, Kpiangbe, Kpiangbe, Kpiangbe. I am coming out, coming out, coming out."*

The rainforest was governed by a tribal council of which *Kpiangbe* was the oldest member. He therefore took advantage of his status in the tribal council to operate an effective, oppressive propaganda and intimidation machinery which ensured that the inhabitants of the rainforest always did his bidding and never stepped out of line, so to speak.

Of all the birds, in the Gola rainforest, the Nightingale had the most melodious voice, and conducted the night choir, with over three hundred different songs in his repertoire. It was therefore no surprise when he was appointed the Town Crier. As Town Crier, it was therefore his duty to announce the times for the tribal rites of passage induction ceremony. It was required by tribal law, to announce the ceremonial rites at least a day before the rites commenced. On the eve of the induction ceremony, Nightingale would catalogue and highlight the history of the rite of passage, and sing the praise of the inductees, in a beautiful compelling voice so as to encourage community support and participation and dispel rumors of fear.

But it was always on this same night that *Kpiangbe*'s propaganda machinery would gear into action and his announced threats and cries of intimidation became malevolent.

"Kpiangbe, Kpiangbe, Kpiangbe, Kpiangbe. I am coming out, coming out, coming out. *Hensinahuayena ngama aye touŋ ngolie a gbwa vavava.* About this time tomorrow, blood will flow;

and pee will spray like a pump. *Kpiangbe, Kpiangbe, Kpiangbe, Kpiangbe.* I am coming out, coming out, coming out."

This was his way of striking fear into the hearts of new inductees and initiates. And every time he screamed his false intimidating cry of what he wanted initiates to read as their death sentence, the whole community, especially the new inductees and initiation candidates would go into a panic-stricken frenzy. They would abandon whatever activities they were engaged in, drop their food in the courtyard, and go into hiding. A couple of hours would go by, before they would feel safe enough to return to their nests or resume their normal activities. Meanwhile, *Kpiangbe* would quickly stagger outside, and gobble up the food abandoned in their hurried flight. He would then quietly retreat to his nest and settle down to digest then regurgitate his meal until another occasion warranted his intimidating outcry of:

Kpiangbe, Kpiangbe, Kpiangbe, Kpiangbe. I am coming out, coming out, coming out. *Kpiangbe, Kpiangbe, Kpiangbe, Kpiangbe.* I am coming out, coming out, coming out. *Kpiangbe, Kpiangbe, Kpiangbe, Kpiangbe.* I am coming out, coming out, coming out.

At which time, the whole tribal community would with one accord, beg *Kpiangbe* in a panic stricken voice, not to come out.

"*Bagbwaa, Konneh Bagbwaa, Bagbwaa, Bagbwaa.*"

Don't come out, please don't come out, don't come out.

"*Bagbwaa, Konneh Bagbwaa, Bagbwaa, Bagbwaa.*"

Don't come out, please don't come out, don't come out

"*Bagbwaa, Konneh Bagbwaa, Bagbwaa, Bagbwaa.*"

Don't come out, please don't come out, and don't come out.

All the inhabitants of the Gola forest came to perceive *Kpiangbe* as a fearful monster and lived in awe of him. Time went by, and *Kpiangbe* continued his intimidation. The birds accepted his bullying tactics, and very soon it became standard practice for them to drop off their food, and go into hiding when they heard what they considered his "insider story" describing the initiation and rite of passage.

For their own peace of mind, the tribal community of the rainforest decided that instead of going into a panic attack every morning, day in and night out, they would rather forage for *Kpiangbe*, drop off his food by his nest, before foraging for themselves and for their young. So without leaving his nest, most of the time, *Kpiangbe* had a constant supply of food. As he grew older, his voice became twice as terrifying and intimidating and so also did his appetite increase. He would often announce his presence and demand for more food in an obscene cacophony of intimidating foul cries and screams.

The Gola rainforest community therefore signed a "memorandum of understanding" with *Kpiangbe* with a clause of appeasement--"feed the beast, keep him quiet and he will not bother us," The animals reasoned. As long as they brought him a constant supply of food, *Kpiangbe* was appeased, and the kingdom knew peace. But it was a fragile peace. The tribal council had created a monster, now it was apparent that if something was not done soon enough, this monster would devour everything in its path. Several years went by, and the status quo was maintained. This was the predicament the Gola rainforest found itself in, until the day the town had an unexpected visitor—a son of the soil in the person of *Jakoi* the House Swallow had returned home.

Jakoi, the House Swallow had been away in a foreign land, learning the ways of the world. On his return home to the Gola rainforest, the elders of the rainforest, including the Old Owl, The Wise Egret, the Stork, Parrot The Orator and Peacock The Proud, had a closed-door meeting with House Swallow who was now considered the most erudite in the whole kingdom.

"A very grave situation developed here, while you were gone. Maybe with your worldly knowledge, you would be able to help us find a solution," the Owl introduced the subject.

"What situation are we talking about, Old One?", *Jakoi* the House Swallow asked.

"Maybe you can be the go-between," The Egret offered.

"Eh hmmmmmm! We have a monster in our midst," a monster in our midst," the Parrot spilled the beans.

"*Tsk, Tsk, Tsk*, don't raise your voice, he may hear us," The Stork admonished in silent fear.

"Now that you are here, *Jakoi*," you are expected to feed the monster a double portion of food, just like the rest of us. And I say this meeting is over, I have to go out and spread out my beautiful plumage before the sun goes down," the proud Peacock announced.

"Not so fast my child. Maybe this son of the land has got an answer for us," the Egret intervened.

"What answer could a mere boy have, other than feed the monster? Peacock replied.

"Let the young man speak," The Egret admonished.

"Thank you Oh Wise One, I may have a solution to the problem, but I must first ask a couple of questions," *Jakoi* the House Swallow replied.

"Go ahead my son," the Owl urged *Jakoi* the House Swallow on.

"I have been told we have a monster in our midst. And that it is my duty to feed this monster like everyone else in this kingdom. Now before I feed the monster, I want to know, what kind of food does this monster eat?" *Jakoi*, the House Swallow asked.

"Oh! He eats berries and fruits like some of us," the Parrot replied.

"And what does this monster look like?" *Jakoi* asked.

What does it matter what he looks like? "We do not know what he looks like. All we know is that he is a monster," the Peacock replied.

"All those who have seen this monster stand on one leg," *Jakoi*, the House Swallow instructed.

Nobody took up the challenge.

"*Mbue* Mr. Owl has seen the monster," The Stork replied.

Mr. Owl, can you tell us what the Monster looks like?" *Jakoi*, the House swallow asked.

"No, I only saw his shadow but I know he is very fearful," The Owl replied.

"Everyone is afraid, so we feed him and beg him to stay in his nest," they replied in chorus.

"So none of you have ever seen this monster?" *Jakoi*, the House Swallow asked. "How many of you know his name?" *Jakoi* the House Swallow questioned.

"We do not know his name, but we call him *Kpiangbe*," they replied in unison.

"Why do you think he is terrorizing the kingdom? Have you ever challenged his motives?" *Jakoi*, the House Swallow asked.

"No, he is a monster; we don't go around questioning monsters. We are afraid of him, so we beg him to stay in his nest and not come outside of his nest to bother us," The peacock replied.

"We are afraid the monster might come out of his big nest and devour everything in his path," the Stork concurred.

"Well I have news for everybody," *Jakoi*, the House Swallow replied.

"Good or bad news," the Parrot piped out.

"If none of you have ever seen the Monster, how do you know he is a monster?" *Jakoi*, the House Swallow asked.

"We can tell he is a monster by the sound of his terrible voice," the others defended.

"If we ever hope to get rid of this monster, we have to know what he looks like," *Jakoi*, the House Swallow challenged.

"How do you suggest we do that?" they asked in panic.

"We have to get the monster out of his nest," *Jakoi*, the House Swallow challenged. "And how do you intend to get the monster out of his nest," they asked.

"Very simple," *Jakoi*, the House Swallow replied. "From this day henceforth, nobody feeds the '*monster*. And if the monster wants to come out of his nest, then let him come out. But there will be no panic, no hiding, no begging or pleading with the monster anymore. From this day henceforth, the monster is free to come out of his nest, anytime he pleases. Do we all agree?" *Jakoi*, the House Swallow challenged.

"Ay! We do agree," they chirruped.

So it was agreed that nobody would so much as talk to the monster, let alone stop him from coming out.

Soon after the meeting *Kpiangbe* went into another frenzy calling out with a loud scream:

"*Kpiangbe, Kpiangbe, Kpiangbe, Kpiangbe*. I am coming out, coming out, coming out. *Hensinahuayena ngama aye touŋ ngolie a gbwa vavava*. About this time tomorrow, blood will flow; and pee will spray like a pump. *Kpiangbe, Kpiangbe, Kpiangbe, Kpiangbe*. I am coming out, coming out, coming out."

This time, there was complete and total silence. *Kpiangbe* screamed, cried, cursed and called out, but the animals neither paid any attention to him nor pleaded or begged him to stay inside his nest.

He flapped his wings, shouted and screamed with all his might in his most intimidating high pitched tone;

"*Kpiangbe, Kpiangbe, Kpiangbe, Kpiangbe*. I am coming out, coming out, coming out. *Hensinahuayena ngama aye touŋ ngolie a gbwa vavava*. About this time tomorrow, blood will flow; and pee will spray like a pump. *Kpiangbe, Kpiangbe, Kpiangbe, Kpiangbe*. I am coming out, coming out, coming out."

The birds paid *Kpiangbe* no attention. Everybody went about their business, and ignored the nuisance with the loud voice.

For the first time, in the history of the Gola forest, *Kpiangbe* was being ignored, and he did not like it. The threats increased, and the screams and shouts became louder and louder.

"*Kpiangbe, Kpiangbe, Kpiangbe, Kpiangbe*. I am coming out, coming out, coming out. *Hensinahuayena ngama aye touŋ ngolie a gbwa vavava*. About this time tomorrow, blood will flow; and pee will spray like a pump. *Kpiangbe, Kpiangbe, Kpiangbe, Kpiangbe*. I am coming out, coming out, coming out."

The elders in the community came to *Jakoi*, the House Swallow in an outburst. "You told us not to go into hiding, but *Kpiangbe* is getting louder and we cannot stand his screams any more. What should we do?" they asked.

"We do nothing," *Jakoi* replied in a firm voice.

"You brought this upon our heads, you do something," the crow challenged.

"Just ignore *Kpiangbe* and let him scream all he can," *Jakoi*, the House Swallow advised.

"For all the years, you have been away, and all the education you say you have acquired, is this all you have to say to us, "do nothing?" the peacock challenged.

"If you want to go into hiding fine, but I am staying right here." *Jakoi*, bantered. The screams and cries went on all night, and the following night. Days went on, and *Kpiangbe*, who loved to listen to his own voice, got out of control, screaming and shouting at the slightest movement.

"Kpiangbe, Kpiangbe, Kpiangbe, Kpiangbe. I am coming out, coming out, coming out. *Hensinahuayena ngama aye touŋ ngolie a gbwa vavava.* About this time tomorrow, blood will flow; and pee will spray like a pump. *Kpiangbe, Kpiangbe, Kpiangbe, Kpiangbe.* I am coming out, coming out, coming out."

Finally, *Jakoi*, the House Swallow had had enough of this intimidation and he called all the birds to gather in front of Egrets nest.

"I have called all of you here, to tell you that the next time *Kpiangbe* screams *"Kpiangbe, Kpiangbe, Kpiangbe"* again we will all respond together with one voice *"Gwaa."* Is that understood?" *Jakoi*, the House Swallow instructed.

"Understood," the others responded.

Soon after the meeting, Kpiangbe went into a tirade of

screams and cries bordering on insults.

"*Kpiangbe, Kpiangbe, Kpiangbe, Kpiangbe.* I am coming out, coming out, coming out. *Hensinahuayena ngama aye touŋ ngolie a gbwa vavava.* About this time tomorrow, blood will flow; and pee will spray like a pump. *Kpiangbe, Kpiangbe, Kpiangbe, Kpiangbe.* I am coming out, coming out, coming out."

Finally the Gola fauna responded with one voice, "*Gwaa, gwaa, gwaa.* Come out, come out, come out."

And out came the odd-looking diminutive, unkempt, scaly, disagreeable, musky odor-smelling, and foul-mouth intimidating screaming midget of a bird. The whole tribal council booed *Kpiangbe* with a chorus symphony of "*Oh-o-o-o-o-o-o-o.*" The shriek of hoarse cries, grunts, growls, hisses, pecking sounds, chirrups and animal laughter were so loud that the mountains, hills and valley echoed their sound in reverse order. They laughed at *Kpiangbe*, teased and taunted him and called him names.

Siaka Kroma

A MAN CALLED SCORPION

Fidelis Tomasi had been appointed the new Anti-Corruption Commissioner of Krukishtan. He was the fourth in a line of Anti-Corruption Commissioners who had failed in their mission for one reason or the other. He was a distinguished lawyer, a no-nonsense man as his colleagues characterized him. The public had dubbed him 'Scorpion'. All hopes for curbing corruption in Krukishtan now lay with him. He was a tall man with a solid frame. Years of regular exercise had endowed him with strong, muscular, and attractive features. He was prepared both in mind and body to take up his new challenge.

Tomasi had studied law in the country's premiere university. He had gone on and studied criminal law at Westminster Law School in London and added civil rights and international law at Harvard to his portfolio. As an overseas student, Fidelis had developed an aversion for the antics of African politicians, politicians who robbed their countries and stashed their loot away in foreign banks. *How can the continent develop with such crooks?* The list was endless: Mabatu of Zanfire Makasa of the Central Bundanda Republic, Sonny Igeda of Nasara, Ngumeh of Southern Guinea and Bindeile of Krukishtan. He noted that leaders of countries with oil and mineral wealth had left their countries impoverished and undeveloped by such acts of wanton greed and impunity. If there was a God in heaven, such vermin should be made to pay for their deeds.

Tomasi read such stories about African leaders with indignation. Even before he had left America to return home to Krukishtan, he had come to the belief that African countries were incapable of cleaning up their own houses; someone needed to do it for them, unpalatable as that sounded. In his strong opinion, such cases should be under the jurisdiction of the International Criminal Court (ICC). *There should be provision for economic crimes to be categorized as crimes against humanity*, he would say to himself.

Tomasi was motivated in his practice by injustice in society and impunity in governance. These two focuses had almost become a crusade for him. He spoke on university campuses and in public about the need to classify economic crimes as crimes against humanity to be prosecuted by the International Criminal Court. It was with such zeal that he approached his new job.

Reaction to Tomasi's appointment was swift, yet mixed.

"At last…!" Some said.

"He will be compromised soon." Others feared.

"Remember the first governor of the central bank?" Some cautioned.

"It will only be a matter of time." Others concluded prophetically.

Tomasi started his new job as he did all others before it. He prayed to God for guidance. In this particular case, he prayed even harder for fortitude, for courage to stand up to the pressure that was sure to come. He prayed for humility, for strength to keep a low profile, to resist the limelight, and the praise singing from the national press that his successors had succumbed to. He prayed for steadfastness in looking out for the weak in a society of powerful men drunken by impunity. This became his daily prayer routine.

That he was a no-nonsense man was not in dispute. For many, the questions were: 'How long would he stay that way? Would he be supported by 'big power' and the courts? Would he be corrupted as others before him?

When Tomasi set to work, results were quick and wholesome. All active cases were vigorously prosecuted without plea deals or loophole fines. His accomplishments were marked by indictment after indictment and conviction after conviction. Newspapers blazed his achievements in glowing headlines: *Fidelis Indicts Minister of Trade; Fidelis Sends Two Judges to Jail for Bribery; Fidelis Ends Culture of Impunity; Jail and Fine for Permanent Secretary*; and more.

Following a year of success, Tomasi felt comfortable in his job. He was succeeding in his job and he was receiving the needed appreciation for it. One morning, he received a call from his senior investigative officer urgently requesting a meeting with him. When they met, his officer was livid with panic. He had been investigating Keju Belleh, a senior government minister, and his wife for involvement in illegal diamond trade and other nefarious activities.

"I need your permission to proceed with this," he blurted out.

"Permission to proceed with what?" He queried exasperatingly.

"It is Dr. Keju Belleh and his wife. We have been investigating them for some time now. The news is not good. We have them in drug trafficking, in illicit diamond and gold deals, in smuggling arms to rebels next door, in demanding bribes from investors and for evading tax."

"Are you sure?"

"Yes Sir. The evidence is solid on all fronts. We can convict both husband and wife with less material than we have on them, Sir."

"So, what is stopping you?"

"Well, you know the minister involved. You know his position in government. I did not want to pursue this without your involvement."

"You want me to take this one over."

"Yes Sir."

"Let me see the material and decide for myself."

He quickly rifled through a pile of evidence that had been cautiously collated in a lever arch file.

"One piece of advice," looking at his officer sternly.

"Yes Sir."

"Not a word outside our trusted circle."

"Yes Sir."

"Don't tell even your wife."

"Yes Sir."

"Make sure that every single document is reproduced in triplicate and kept in three separate locations, including outside the office building. Have everything scanned and stored digitally and let me have my own copies as soon as you finish them."

"Yes Sir."

"Okay. Good luck and have a nice day."

"Have a nice day, Mr. Tomasi."

For ten days, Scorpion locked himself in his office and pored over the documents as he received them from his chief investigating officer. He made up his mind to take up the case. The evidence was too strong against the minister, his wife, and their associates. Going over the case, all the anger he had always felt against public officials who milk the economies of their countries accounting for poverty and underdevelopment became ever more palpable. He owed it to the country and his people to pursue this case and through it, clean up the system some more as well as set the right examples.

Memories of similar cases of impunity flashed through his mind: the bank governor rumoured to have been murdered for refusing the president; the spate of killings by government security agents that had gone unpunished; the mountain of inquiry reports whose recommendations had been swept under the carpet, or were accumulating dust and mildew in sealed boxes. He swore to himself that this would be the exception.

The case began with furore: Newspapers, radio stations, and the national television, all carried it and reported it several times that day. All sorts of analyses were made. Public reaction was in solidarity with the new NACA Prosecutor. In phone-in programs, callers expressed disgust, *Dɛm pipul ya dɔn pas mak* (meaning, these people have exceeded their limit).

The minister's wife and their associates were arrested on a Friday evening and held in remand till Monday morning, when they would appear before a presiding magistrate to enter their pleas. The minister had mysteriously escaped this hauling in. Rumour was that he had been tipped off on his way home from his office; that he had not been able to warn his wife; that he had simply directed his driver to drive to his village. He turned himself in an hour before the hearing on the Monday morning.

The courtroom was full to the gallery. The accused were brought in shortly before the judge appeared. The court clerk read out the charges. All pleaded not guilty. The prosecutor and the defence proceeded to make cases for and against bail. Tomasi argued that the accused should be held in remand as the investigation was still in progress. He argued that if released, the accused would tamper with witnesses and jeopardise the entire investigation. He cited the status of the minister and the fact that he had eluded arrest the previous Friday. The defence countered that all the accused had no previous criminal involvement and were reputable members of society. They explained that the minister was not available the previous Friday simply because he was visiting his loyal constituents over the weekend and had turned himself in promptly upon his return to the city.

The defence argued that a person like the minister had too much to lose. All had no flight risk and should be allowed bail. In his ruling, the magistrate agreed with the defence that the minister and his wife posed no flight risk. He therefore granted them self-bail. In the matter of the associates, the magistrate ruled that the possibility of flight existed. He therefore denied bail and returned them to remand. The case was adjourned till the 15th of the following month, thirty days from the initial hearing.

Tomasi was furious at the magistrate's verdict in the matter of bail. In his reckoning, this was an instance of differential justice: *protect the powerful, sacrifice the powerless.* Phone-in callers agreed with his position over the airwaves. *Na di smɔl wan dɛm dɛm kin ketch; 'dɛm de frai di smɔl fish, di kuta im escape. Na so we de oh, na Krukishtan. Yu we nɔ get, na yu de go jeil. Na dɔn da kes dɔn dɔn so.*

In the days following, Tomasi worked very hard to prepare his case. He now saw it his responsibility that the weak in remand were cared for and would get a fair treatment in the trial. He also went over the details of the preliminary hearing. It could mean only one thing: influence was at work. Big influence was at work. He resolved he would do his best to obtain a conviction, especially for the minister and his wife. If in the end he believed that justice was thwarted, he would resign his position. He would not stay in a job that prosecuted the weak and protected the powerful.

One night, two weeks after the preliminary hearing of 'State vs. Dr. Keju Belleh and others', Tomasi stayed late in his office. Around 8:00 O'clock he prepared to go home; he called his wife to say he was on his way home. He locked his office, said good night to the security officer in charge of keeping watch and stepped into his car. As he left the driveway to enter the main road, he noticed two cars on either side of his driveway but paid no heed to them. He had not driven far when one car overtook him and slowed down to a stop. He tried to reverse in order to pass the car that had blocked his way. Another car had blocked him at the back. Two men approached him and ordered him out of his car. He was about to protest when they showed him two guns pointing at him from both his left and right.

"Leave the key in the car and come out quietly?"

"Don't do anything stupid; you won't be hurt."

His mind went to all the cases of armed robbery that appeared in the courts every day. He had been advised that in the event of an armed robbery, one should simply comply with the robbers' demands to avoid being hurt. He now complied. One man took him to the car in front. The other went into his car and drove it back. He was not to know but it was abandoned right in his driveway. He was placed between two people in the back seat.

"Mr. Tomasi, do as you are told and you will not be hurt."

They pulled a hood over his head and told him to lie back. Tomasi did. The car sped away, windows rolled up, air conditioning up high, and music blaring. Above it all, his mind was racing through the clues his investigative mind had equipped him with. *These could not be armed robbers. They know my name. This is either about money or a case I am handling, possibly the one involving the minister.* He concluded that they must want him alive. He was therefore not in any danger of losing his life. With that conclusion, he relaxed somewhat as they drove him in circles till he lost his orientation.

At last the car stopped in a quiet location. He was led out of the car into a building, down a flight of stairs into a room. He was seated at a table. His hood was still on. He could feel that the air-conditioner was switched on. He also suspected that his escorts were waiting for something or someone. Soon, he heard footsteps. More people entered the room. The hood was removed from his head. There, seated at the same table but opposite him, was the minister he had indicted two weeks prior. He saw a gun on the table where he sat. Yards away from the table, stood uniformed members of the notorious National Security Unit, a secret paramilitary force that intimidated people who opposed government. This force operated largely from the shadows and was dreaded by the citizens who had dubbed it the 'WSU', acronyms for '*We Shoot U*'. It was notoriously trigger happy.

Its presence had been strenuously denied by the government. Scores of journalists were paid by government to deny its presence, to sanitize its activities, and to attribute its actions to those of the regular police force.

Fidelis and the minister looked at each other for a long minute or two, without words. Then the minister started.

"Let us cut out the pretences and niceties, Mr. Tomasi. No one knows you are here. You cannot be traced to this place. I know you have a wife and two children. I will be generous with you."

He paused and waved his hands at one of the NSUs in the room. The officer left and returned with a bottle of Martell Cordon Bleu and two glasses. The minister opened it rather ostentatiously. He proceeded to the door and poured a libation.

"To those who have gone before us..." He paused. "And those who may soon join them."

He returned to the table and poured drinks into the two glasses. He pushed one glass toward Tomasi and took a large swig himself, with relish.

"Drink!" He ordered Tomasi.

"I don't drink alcohol." He lied.

"I said 'drink!'." He said again, this time in a menacing tone. Tomasi sensed the vitriol in his voice.

"But, I don't drink alcohol; it's haram to me." Tomasi said stubbornly.

"You are not playing games with me, are you? You are disobeying me. I'll show you."

He turned to the officer on the right of Tomasi and nodded his head to him. The officer approached Tomasi and made as if he was reaching for the glass. In a blinding flash he gave

Tomasi a slap so heavy that it echoed in the room. It knocked Tomasi off his chair. The officer to his left helped him back into his chair, where he sat facing the minister, still dazed by the force of the blow to his face.

"Let's not play games, Mr. Tomasi. Don't insult my generosity. Now drink!"

"I don't drink." Tomasi again stubbornly responded.

Again the minister tilted his head, this time to his left. Tomasi fixed his gaze on the officer who had slapped him. When the blow came, it came from his left, from the officer who had helped him to the chair after falling off. Now he fell to the right of the chair. The first officer approached him to help him get up. Tomasi made it to the chair before he got to him.

"Drink, Mr Tomasi. Drink!" The minister rose up slowly. "You are trying my patience."

Tomasi quickly assessed his situation. It was precarious, to say the least. Here he was in no man's land, no one knew where he was; he could die here and no one would know what happened to him. His wife, his children would not know. Fear slowly crept through him. His family needed him, alive. He reluctantly reached for the glass of cognac. He held it in his hand, struggling to keep his hand steady; struggling to disguise his fear. The minister knew the signs too well to miss them now. He stood patiently to allow Tomasi the dignity of lifting the glass to his own mouth. He sat down when Tomasi took his first reluctant sip.

"Not bad, eh?" the Minister asked. Tomasi did not answer. "Drink more!" The minister urged.

Tomasi took another sip.

"Now let's get back to business. We want you to leave this

case. We want you to withdraw all charges."

"I cannot. It is no longer in my hands. It is with the prosecution lawyers. It is their decision now, they and the judges, not mine..."

"Don't think I am such a fool. All we want is your acquiescence. If you promise not to do anything about it, the matter will be dropped. Witnesses will recount their stories, documents will disappear, judges will recuse themselves, the chief justice will reassign the case to a compliant judge; and all will be well. You would not have lifted a finger. All you do is, turn a blind eye."

Tomasi sat, deep in thought, going over the minister's words in his mind: *the matter will be dropped. Witnesses will recount their stories, documents will disappear, judges will recuse themselves, the chief justice will reassign the case to a compliant judge; and all will be well. You would not have lifted a finger. All you do is turn a blind eye.* He was seeing some clarity. This is how his successors had failed. This is how the wheel turns.

"There is money in the envelope in front of you; lots of money, in dollars. I know your worth, Scorpion, so I have not insulted you by undervaluing you. You can take the money and walk out of that door a free man, or the boys here will give you the usual treatment we mete out to recalcitrant people like you, and you will not be heard about again."

He thought about his wife and two children. They needed a father. He thought about his unfinished house project. He thought about his principles, about all he had stood for in life. But what good is your principle when you are dead? His countrymen did not appreciate heroes. They prefer politicians with deep pockets who lie to them during elections and keep them in penury afterwards. He decided he would accept the bribe. He would accept the bribe just this time. He would hit back at the system by promptly resigning and moving overseas.

Unknown to Tomasi, two plain clothes policemen had quietly entered the room. The minister walked to where Tomasi sat. He took the envelope from the table and thrust it in Tomasi's face. Tomasi read his gesture to mean, 'Take it or else.' And he knew what the 'or else' meant. He took the envelope from the minister.

"You have ruined me." Tomasi managed to say through misty eyes as he accepted the envelope.

"More than you know." The minister replied callously. "Give him the goodbye with the compliments of the President." He said to the agents in the room as he walked out of the room.

"You are under arrest, Mr. Tomasi, for demanding a bribe from a government minister."

The officers handcuffed Tomasi and placed a hood over his head. They put him in a sealed van and took him to a secret building in the city for *questioning*. They led him through a maze of stairs to a dungeon in the basement of the building. They gave him a statement to sign. He refused. He was not going to sign a statement he had not written. The officers proceeded to torture him.

First, they let him stand face against the wall, his head still hooded. They took turns to twist his arms tightly behind his back till they could hear the bones cracking.

"Now, there is more of that treatment. You don't need that. Just sign the statement and we will let you go."

Tomasi again refused.

Then they brought out the *Kobokos* (dried cow hide specially treated for torture). They beat him with their *Kobokos* till he passed out. Then they revived him and told him to sign the document. Still he refused. The police officers got irritated. They decided to elevate the torture to what they jokingly referred to as *third floor treatment*.

"Okay Mr. Stubborn Clever, we'll give you the VIP treatment. We'll give you the third floor treatment."

This stage was horrible. They suspended Tomasi from the ceiling, connected electric wires to his fingers, toes, and genitals. They would apply intermittent jolts of electricity. At the first jolt, Tomasi screamed out loud, as his body convulsed from waves of pain. After the second and subsequent doses, his body fought violently as each jolt threw him into more spasms. He must have lost consciousness.

When he woke up, Tomasi found himself in his wife's arms shaking and sweating.

"You have had a very restless night."

"You have no idea."

He kissed his wife, got out of bed, poured himself a stiff glass of whisky, shook his head, sat down and wrote this story.

Moses Kainwo

THE THIEF

It was about 3:00 p.m. when a young man in blue French suit stood in the window of a female teacher's flat. The teacher had just stepped outside leaving her eight-year old ward behind to watch her favourite comedian on video. The young man had locked the front and back doors of the first floor of the staff quarters of the school.

"I'm not a thief," the man helplessly defended himself.

"Well, what are you doing in a house that is not yours at this time of day?" one of the boys on the lawn shouted back. He was carrying a stone bigger than his own head in his hand, determined to crush the head of the thief whenever the latter decided to step outside.

"I'm not a thief!"

"You are not a thief but who are you? No one in this compound knows you."

"I'm not a thief! You will get to know me if only you are patient to find out."

"Tell us who you are," shouted an elderly woman, a teacher. She waved a long kitchen knife over her head with a threat, "I will castrate you for your mother today. By the way what have you done to that little girl? Can we see her?"

"Of course she is quite safe here with me. I could not let you people hurt her with the missiles you have been throwing at me. Yes, you will see her. She is safe!"

Somebody once said that books did not create wisdom but that wisdom created books. The most illiterate chief in the village has shown his extent of wisdom from his method of handling cases brought to him on a daily basis. The driver of a car has shown it through her nervous responses to unexpected challenges on the road on the spur of the moment. The neglected housewife has shown it through her manipulation of figures for shopping at the market to make ends meet for her thick-skinned husband. The pilot will maneuver her plane to acceptable heights to obtain maximum result. The 4-1-9ers have their special school for lending wisdom to the novice—their kind and the other kind.

Solomon (called Solo for short among friends) was one of the most brilliant students of his class and so no one was surprised when he graduated with a first class honours degree in engineering. He became the talk of the college and the radios. He was of course the pride of his lecturers.

One thing troubled Solo though—he needed a girlfriend that could evolve into a life-long partner. Many had let him down and so he was not so sure whom to trust. Sylvia's parents would have none of that for their only daughter. According to her parents she should have at least two Masters Degrees before thinking of a boyfriend let alone marriage. This was the sanction both Sylvia and Solo had to surmount. Because of that they decided they could marry at the Registry quietly without the knowledge of Sylvia's parents—Solo had lost his own parents just before he turned thirteen. At twenty three he went ahead and got married to Sylvia, a graduate like himself. She had just celebrated her twenty-first birthday.

Solo's parents had died in a fire accident at home. He and his sister Kadi` had left a lighted candle in the study when they went to bed. At about 2:00 a.m. everybody woke up to the fire and had the chance to escape death. Solo's parents were busy looking for money and property which the fierce fire did not permit. When their parents died Kadi was sixteen years old. Their uncle took over their responsibility. He took them into his home where he and his two wives already had seven children between them. What people did not know was that the house Mr. Kuyateh and his wives lived in was property that belonged to his late sister Salamatu, the mother of Kadi and Solomon. The lawyer that had information on the will decided not to announce the details of who the property belonged to as no one else had stepped forward to take charge of the children. He planned to do so now that the children were grown up.

Mr. Kuyateh was the cause of Kadi's leaving school so early when he turned her into his third wife secretly. The girl knew it was wrong but could not protest as that would mean the end of care for her and her brother. He found reason to send his wives out whenever he wanted the girl. He would ask one to cash money for him at a distant bank (where his friend worked as manager), and ask the other to go to the market to prepare some special dish for him. Knowing that all the doors were locked, he would start chasing Kadi all over the place until he trapped her, often times in the kitchen. Then he would threaten to kill her after grabbing a kitchen knife or some other tool. If the girl said she was menstruating he would say,

"What about your behind? Many people are known to enjoy anal sex these days."

"Okay," Kadi normally responded. "Do you want me now?"

"Oh, sure! That's my favourite niece. You seem to be learning so fast. I think I should let you know that I've grown to prefer your back to your front."

"What makes you different from homosexuals?"

"They have gone public with their trade. In fact they have become so religious about it, that I hate to associate myself with them."

"But Uncle, regardless of what you say I want you to know that you don't really love me. You are determined to destroy my future. Now that I know this is what you are determined to achieve, I give myself to you because I can't beat you at your game especially when I continue to stay under your roof. The only thing I will say is that I won't let you have sex with me if you are not using the condom. Your behaviour is very unsafe. Two wives are not enough for you and I'm sure you do try your luck with other women at your office. And look at what you are doing to me, an orphan you are supposed to protect."

Whether the girl menstruated or not he would only go to sleep after a good sex session with her. His favourite starter was always the nipples. He would suck her nipples so voraciously that he would beat a six-month old at her hungry grab of breast for breast milk. And then sitting on a bench in the kitchen with the girl sobbing in a corner he went on to say,

"I really should not be doing this to you. But I love you and if you allow me I will marry you."

"Not me, no! You turned me into a whore. What should I be doing with a sixty-five-year-old?"

"You don't remember what you did just now? You gave me peace of mind when you allowed me to have sex with you."

"I was under duress. You know it. You raped me!"

When she found a promising boyfriend at the age of eighteen, her uncle threw her out of the house but her brother continued to stay there. Her boyfriend decided to marry her on her nineteenth birthday. Their uncle and his wives refused to attend the wedding saying she was too young to get married. Solo felt more comfortable living with his sister than with his uncle. Besides, Mr. Kuyateh did not look after Solo and his sister the same way he cared for his children. When he accused them of bad manners, he was only condemning his own children. When he accused them of laziness, he was merely recalling the behavior of his own children. When he called them thieves, he only echoed what the neighbours knew his children to be.

Sylvia grew up under very strict conditions. Her parents, Mr. and Mrs. Thompson, would not let their daughter go out of the house once she arrived home from college. They got her to learn how to drive at the age of nineteen but would only allow her to drive them to the beach on the last Sunday of every month when they went for lunch at one of the beach restaurants. At the restaurant she was given the opportunity to choose what they would have for lunch. She ordered humus her favourite starter before asking for fish and chips.

"Sylvia?"

"Yes Papa," Sylvia would sound suspicious at such times.

"You seem never to get tired of this stuff. You want the same dish every time we come here. Your Mum and I have observed that for quite some time now you only order fish and chips."

"But Papa, you and Mama are free to order something else. I just want to make sure I don't ask for what we normally have at home. I keep telling myself that any time I come out I should have something special. Usual is trivial after a trip to the top of Everest."

"Do you call this outing Everest?" Her Mum was not sure why this expression.

"Oh yes, Mama. This is a monthly event and so it is not usual. It is like one trying to climb Mount Everest once in a while."

"I don't have a problem with that as long as you work hard at your books," said Mr. Thompson.

"But why don't you allow me to drive the car and go where I wish to go alone? Sometimes I just want to be on my own to reflect on life."

"Oh you will do that once you get married probably ten years from now."

"There you go again. Papa, how would you feel if I decided to marry someone of my choice secretly knowing that I now have my first degree—without your knowledge of course, since you might never permit me to do so at this stage?" Sylvia was always careful not to give away her secret marriage to someone from the country, a "savage" (in the subconscious of her parents). This would be the worst of ten evils in this family.

"Simple—we will just disown you."

"Disown me your only child?"

"Yes. There are many children waiting to be adopted."

"Mama and Papa, I didn't know you to be authoritarian.

Are you sure you are not going to mess up my future? Did you listen to your own voice when you spoke just now? It seems I am only a toy in your hands—your happiness is best achieved when you toss me about like a puppet. From what you say I am sure you even want to choose my life partner. That's where I'm going to fall out with you people." She recalls that the only witness to their wedding was Kadi, Solo's elder sister.

"Let's not talk about that here. We will cross the bridge when we get there," said her father.

Solo's visit to Sylvia was to celebrate their wedding quietly while Sylvia's parents were at work. Normally they would not be home until 9 or 10 p.m. So Sylvia and Solo had a field day. They both sat and relaxed on the balcony that overlooked the garden at the back of the house. They played the cool gospel music of Don Moen and enjoyed the special food that Sylvia had prepared. There was roast meat. There was smoked fish. There was *oleleh*. There was *foorah*. There was cassava to go with beans. There was ginger beer. There was *bissap*. African food all the way.

Sylvia was able to wear her wedding ring only when she and Solo were together with no one else around to poke. Apart from avoiding the venom of her parents, she did not forget that she held an executive position in the Christian group where they met in college. She was very careful not to expose their status as married couple without the consent of her parents. In sum they were an underground couple. What she did not know was that on one of those occasions when they had sex the condom was broken and they did not even realize it. She was pregnant already.

"I know we have not gone wrong."

"No. We can't be wrong," said Solo. "If we are wrong, then Abraham and Sarah were wrong."

"No. We can't be wrong. "If we are, then Jacob and Rachel were woefully wrong."

"What about Samson and Delilah?"

"What about Joseph and Mary?" She was so sure of this couple so she went on, "God endorsed their marriage to the extent that He allowed them the gift of His Son to the world."

"You know what? I never saw it like that."

"In fact, Adam and Eve were right until they messed up."

"Absalom was never never right and to make matters worse he messed up with his father's ten concubines."

"We should share scripture before you go home today," Sylvia was so much in love.

"What do you suggest we read?" asked Solo.

"Anything from Songs of Solomon. You will have to rise up to the meaning of your name. Solomon in the Bible was a poet—you ought to be one too. You should be a writer of love songs."

"Honey, thank you. You always challenge me about my capacity to write. I'm going to take it seriously."

They decided to look at their plan for eloping to Europe or America. They were sure that if someone helped them with scholarship, they could go and further their studies abroad and never come back. In all the places they asked, there was prospect for one person to go abroad, not a couple. They agreed that Sylvia should be the first to fly out and they would work on the arrangements for Solo to join her there.

Mr. Thompson, an airlines official, was now at the last stage of the secret plan to celebrate their daughter's twenty-second birthday. He and his wife decided they were going to surprise Sylvia with a ticket to the United Kingdom to read a masters degree in civil engineering. Previously he had assisted his daughter to apply to several colleges abroad without any conclusion. This time he had actually gone on to conclude the matter by paying the fees for a two-year course.

He and his wife spent the better part of the day trying to get a good ticket for their daughter on a good airline.

"I am going to miss her more than you."

"Why should you even think that? I am a woman and she is my daughter."

"Have you not heard that girls are closer to their fathers? The girl hasn't even left and yet I find myself crying secretly almost every night in the bathroom."

"Well her going away should not depend on our feelings. We want to give her the best, a sort of ticket to civilization, something that would prepare her for a good footing in life."

Mr. Thompson gave his wife a broad smile, "You know what? We should not let her come for holidays until she has grabbed her doctorate degree. What I will do is to secure our own ticket to go for summer holidays next year. Alternately, we could both accompany her now but not think of visiting her next year. What do you think?"

"Both sound good to me. However, I believe it will be better for us to visit her next year. For now you should accompany her and hand her over to the college authorities properly—she is Papa's child, I agree."

"Ok, if you say so."

"You had a suggestion about organizing her next birthday at the Cape Sierra Hotel two weeks from now and I was wondering whether we could not save some of that money."

"Well, she still has up to two months to process her visa and I thought until then her stay with us should be eventful. Her birthday is one such event."

"I agree but we don't have to be elaborate," said Mrs. Thompson.

"She has been very good so we should outdo her goodness with our generosity. She deserves it! The manager at the hotel was impressed that we wanted this for our daughter so he gave me a lot of concession on the cost."

"Ok, let's go for it. Thanks."

Sylvia was going to remind Solo not to be late for the family meeting where a lawyer was going to read the will his father had left behind. Sylvia came out of the bathroom and was combing her hair when the front gate of their compound opened. She was not sure of the sound she heard so she tried to find out. Solo had seen Mr. and Mrs. Thompson drive in through the main gate and had taken a big jump at the back and was now busy climbing the barbed-wire fence to land in a next door neighbour's compound. Both Mr. and Mrs. Thompson raised an alarm together, "Thief!" Sylvia joined the chorus that rang out for the attention of the neighbours and the idle street boys and girls.

Solo was also shouting, "Thief!" as he ran so that the people he met did not know who the real "thief" was. He entered a school compound with the crowd following him until he entered a female teacher's flat. The teacher had gone down the drive to buy some bread for the evening and left her eight-year old ward in the house. Solo knew the compound well because he was a regular visitor to a friend there. But Joseph was not at home. He came back to find people throwing missiles at a thief who stood in the kitchen window of the flat earlier mentioned.

Joseph himself threw stones twice before realizing that it was the face of his friend, Solo. He announced to everyone that it was his friend and not a thief. He spoke to his friend and asked that he opened the front door for him so he could verify the reason for the chaos. Solo opened the door for his friend, his saviour. They spent some fifteen minutes talking before deciding to come out. The girl was the first to step out and she ran straight down into the arms of her aunty. The stones started falling when the people saw the two young men coming out arm-in-arm. Joseph stood on the verandah to introduce his friend to the crowd.

"This is Solo, my friend for over ten years now. He has visited me here several times but mostly he came at night so people in this compound might not know him. He was visiting with his girlfriend in Becklyn Drive. The girl's parents would harm him if they saw him because they do not approve of their daughter having a boyfriend until she is thirty, about ten years from now. In fact they consider him a savage since he comes from the country. The parents returned home much earlier than usual and the only option he had was to flee for dear life. Because they shouted 'Thief!', everybody else shouted, 'Thief!' and that was how he got here." By this time Mr. and Mrs. Thompson had arrived in the compound and were standing at the back of the crowd being addressed.

Gbanabom Hallowell

VIRTUAL INTENTION

"I only have three minutes left, I have to go."

The response to her typescript on the computer screen was delayed for thirty seconds before it came popping up. All the while Maneta's index finger unconsciously tapped the edge of the keyboard.

"What? Why? Just when it was beginning to get interesting?"

"I have to go! I only paid for thirty minutes, and you and I only became friends five minutes ago; since that time you have not said anything. You don't even have your picture on your wall. How do I know you are real?"

"Why don't we start from there?"

"No time for that right now. I am in a public cafe and my time is up." Her fingers typed the last sentence faster than ever. She could hear her own keys being pounded more noisily than the other keyboards in the room.

"Nor broke am oh!"

She refused to be intimidated by that interference.

"Sign back in and..."

The screen blanked out. In three seconds it turned sky blue and a small window appeared with the command for her to sign in. She sat back, heaved a big sigh and stared at the screen. She felt a hand on her shoulder. She didn't show any emotion, because she knew what the hand on her shoulder signified.

"Alright, alright, I know, I know, you rogues." she panted.

"You know, and you always have to wait for me to inform you that someone else is waiting to use the computer, or for the screen to go blank on you?"

"Don't shout at me, you must appreciate the fact that I am a regular customer at your cafe."

"Then you must know better than to always pay for thirty minutes if you want to stay for a whole hour!"

From a back room, the owner's voice quickly came to Maneta's rescue before she and the attendant went into their usual exchange, but not without her throwing the usual reminder that if she had enough money she had the nerve to stay on the computer for up to five hours. She also noted that one day she would have her own laptop and pay for her own internet service to be enjoyed from the comfort of her home and not have the misfortune to bump into good-for-nothing people like the attendant.

At home in her bed, Maneta found time to think over her cyber encounter with her new Facebook friend. The most outstanding aspect of her memory of him was his unfinished sentence before the computer logged her out and turned blank blue.

What was he trying to say before the screen froze? She thought. Was it for her to hear what he had to say about her pictures on her wall? Maneta always wanted to know what her male friends thought of her many pictures on her Facebook wall. In fact, she had just uploaded a few photos before she saw the red prompter alerting her to a new request for friendship. She had quickly clicked on it, and up came the friend, but with no photo on his profile. She was always displeased to have to see a blank wall when men requested friendships with her online.

Her first question to him, after accepting his friendship was where he lived apart from the virtual world. It was in the country of her dreams! *America*! She felt pleased to confirm it in the name she preferred: *the USA?*

"Yes, in the USA," her new friend typed.

"What state?" She asked.

"New York."

"Wow! I love New York."

"Have you been to New York before?"

"No, I have never been out of my country!" She quickly typed as if to erase some mistake she might have made to her new friend. Then she added, "What nationality are you?

"I am a Virtualite!"

"You are funny," Maneta responded. "What nationality is Virtualite?"

"I come from the back waters of the UN Building in Manhattan."

"*Mmmm*, that's fine for you," Maneta wrote smiling. "That should make you an American."

That was the conversation that had taken place between them in the five minutes they had become friends on Facebook. But she did not readily show any eagerness for the new friendship like she had done for the many others with whom she was either currently chatting or had chatted with before she *unfriended* them, for wasting her time and the little credit she struggled to raise to pay to access the Internet. Men are all the same, she maintained. They always want to discuss the sexuality of women. All of the friends she had made; both the ones she initiated and the ones who came after her had insisted on her taking photos of her nudity, and posting them to their personal email addresses.

These men came from all over the world: black men, white men, brown men, and even men without any proper racial colors.

She hadn't realized how much she had gone into thought over her newfound cyber friend until her door was rudely kicked in. A lady, in the worst of moods entered and stood firmly on her legs with arms on her hips as she hissed.

"I am not leaving without my money!" she barked.

"*Umu!* You don't have to do this. I will pay you as soon as I have the money," Maneta pleaded.

"Every day you will pay me...you will pay me; *Me*? I cannot accept that today *oh*! I too have my own problems. It is three weeks now! Each time I ask, you lie to me that someone is sending you money from abroad. *Today,* I need my money. You have money to go and pay Bampia to enter his Internet, but you don't have money to pay me."

"What's your own in my internet business?"

"I need my money *oh*, or I will not leave this place today."

"I don't have money today *oh*; you have to wait until I go to town tomorrow and come back."

"Maneta, I cannot wait another minute."

"But I do not have it now."

"You will have to give me my money."

Umu dashed for the only valuable shoes that Maneta had and was making her way out when Maneta reached for the door and shut it before her. They struggled for some time until they ripped one of the shoes apart. Maneta, frustrated, fell down on the floor and cried like a baby. Satisfied that she had made a point about how desperate she was for her money, Umu dropped one of the pair, and dashed out of the door with the other, swearing that Maneta would not have the other shoe until her every penny of the debt was paid off.

Maneta lived with her daughter in a backyard room. The compound was crowded with tenants, including Umu. At least ten one room apartments were littered all over the unkempt compound. The atmosphere was perpetually suffocating with the etching stench from the outside toilet. Whenever there was mass cooking, the atmosphere became extremely suffocating by the mixed aroma from the single shared kitchen. Maneta's five year old daughter only came into her room to sleep at night. She roamed the compound all day in the company of other kids. Luckily for them in the compound, all mothers were one mother, one mother was all mothers.

Maneta did not cry because of the shoe that Umu ripped, but because of the fact that on that day she had not a penny's worth to her name. She was hungry, her daughter was hungry, and she had spent the last penny she had to access the Internet. An Indonesian Facebook friend had faithfully promised her that because she had sent him the image he wanted to see of her, she was now entitled to his generosity. When she logged in the next time she would receive a message with a code and directions on how to collect a fifty dollar note from an exchange bureau in town. The message never showed up nor was the Indonesian friend signed in. The only consolation she had, if it was ever a consolation, was meeting with the new friend who said he was a Virtualite.

She heard a knock on the door. A male voice introduced himself but she did not show any excitement. She however invited him in. Abibu entered her room. He stood for a while before helping himself to a corner of the bed. For a moment he was silent, and Maneta did not demonstrate any interest in having a conversation. Abibu heard Maneta's daughter crying outside. He quickly dashed out and returned with the child. After then Maneta raised her head to make conversation as if she had only noticed him. Abibu took a piece of bread from his handbag and gave it to the child, who, in accepting it, also accepted his pacification to stop crying. He took the child and put her on his lap. Between sobs and hiccups, the child began to chew the bread. After a while, Abibu allowed the child to come down from his lap. Maneta gave her some water to drink and allowed her to dash out in high spirits, to play with the other children outside. Maneta shut the door after her and returned to the bed.

"What do you want with us?" she asked.

"Why are you asking that? You know I was away visiting the village and I just returned to hear you and Umu fighting over nothing."

"I didn't think you cared. If you cared you would want to know that I had nothing to eat at home before you went AWOL."

Abibu chuckled before he spoke again. "But you know that my wife…"

"*Ah! Ah!* I don't want to hear anything about your wife, please!"

Abibu shut up.

After a brief while he dipped his hands into his pockets and retrieved a wad of notes. "This is for you."

Maneta sluggishly accepted the money, and to her surprise, it was such an impressive bundle.

"Hay, na watin dem dae kill tiday? And she sat upright beaming

with a smile as she examined the wad.

Abibu leaned back on the bed as he stared at the ceiling. Maneta embraced him.

"I have repaid Umu the money you owed her; and here is your shoe that she took from you."

"*Na wae you get plenty for waste na dat make!*" Maneta sucked on her teeth at length, detaching herself from Abibu in mock anger.

"She asks me for money, and I don't treat her like that. Why should she treat me like I am an un-paying debtor?"

"Okay, forget about it now."

Abibu edged himself properly on the bed to be at par with Maneta who still had her head resting on the upper pillow. The two of them smiled at each other before Abibu slid under the sheets to join her.

Maneta paid for thirty minutes and was given a computer shortly after another client had vacated it. She signed her temporary entry code, and opened her Facebook page. The internet was slow, but she was ready to wait forever. After a while she was finally on Facebook. None of the messages was from her new friend. She decided to open the messages she had received. Suddenly, the icon for her new friend's message box popped up. Excitedly, she clicked on it.

"You slept with someone yesterday" the message read. "With a dark man," it added.

Maneta giggled, her face contorting. She quickly turned and looked around to see if anyone was reading her screen or reading her mind.

"What does this mean?" she typed.

"I mean you had sex with a man yesterday at your place."

"Are you joking or what?" she typed again.

"*Ahaahahaha!* I got you!"

"Why would you even think about that?" Maneta questioned.

"Because I know when people I care about cheat on me."

"You are funny. You and I don't even know each other yet."

"I know you now, even though you are not using the same computer in which we met."

"Oh, *please*. How could you know that?"

"I just know."

"Oh, I know, you are one of those I.T. geeks whose lives are all computers, right?"

"That's our life in Virtual Land."

"*Virtual Land* indeed," she typed, instinctively rolling her eyes.

Now comfortable with the conversation, she convinced herself that her new friend had to be the funny kind of guy. She even poked a joke at him that she knew he was sitting in his cozy room with an American girl. The new friend didn't respond to her on that. Instead when his message came again, it was to enquire as to why she had so many photos on Facebook.

"Oh, oh, someone is getting jealous!" Maneta replied.

The chatting continued on the funny thread it started. Maneta was engrossed and kept smiling, at times even laughing aloud, drawing other clients' attention to herself. Each moment, Maneta, becoming more comfortable, chatted about everything she ever imagined America to be. She wanted to know about the kind of grass that grew there and the type of earth that made up the ground; she wanted to know about African Americans. She wanted to know what he had for breakfast, and what he was going to have for dinner; she wanted to know whether he had a big car, the likes that she always saw driven by 'big men', around Freetown. Finally, she told him she was eager to know what he looked like.

"Don't you know what I look like after all this while?" her friend questioned.

"How can I know when your picture is not on your page?"

"Are you sure it is not there? Go to my profile."

Maneta clicked to access his profile. At once there was the faint image of an innocent face, the most attractive face of any man she had ever seen. His eyes glowed with what appeared to be a golden dust of stars. They looked romantic, but at the same time intimidating. She felt as though his eyes transmitted an electrifying shock into her, creating an intense feeling of fatigue all over her body. Maneta intermittently had to avoid his eyes. It was as if they were drying up the wetness in her eyes. She convinced herself that her new friend could only be described as *a beautiful man*.

Just then, the computer screen blinked, and returned with the blue sky, and with the now irritating command for her to sign in anew. She hit the desk with her fist. And just as she was about to leave the seat, the computer hissed. She heard it but she did not pay any attention to it; all she was trying to avoid was the attendant's badmouthing. However, as she rose, the hissing sounded a little louder. She saw the screen playing between colors, and then, her Facebook page reappeared.

Her friend's message came through. Hesitantly, she stared closely at the screen as if she were only seeing it for the first time. Then, peering about her, she slowly returned to her seat.

Her friend had to be a computer wizard indeed! She had heard about those I.T. experts who could hack through any hidden passwords, access any computer and destroy them with viruses. This was going to be a really good game on that good-for-nothing attendant who would not leave her in peace.

"Don't ask me how I did it, just go on and chat with me."

"I am not going to ask you any question on this one. That should be a good one, Mr. I.T. Wizard."

"I'm glad you know my name. I am the Wizard of Oz."

"Is that your nickname?"

"No, it is my real name."

"Ok, Mr. Hardy let's play the game."

"Oh yeah, let's play."

From the corner of her eyes, Maneta saw the attendant passing by her desk. She tried to ignore him while in fear that he could just have realized what had happened to the computer she was using; but the attendant only slowly walked by and instead went to trouble a nearby client. Why hadn't he bothered her that her thirty minutes were over—to think that he was not even countenancing her? What was pushing him away from her? Usually, if she had managed to buy credit for an hour, he would taunt her after the first thirty minutes, exactly when it was running past it. And here she was, two hours later, and still the attendant, going past her several times did not even, as much as tap her shoulder.

"You are lucky I have taken the attendant off your back."

"Wait a minute, how come you know everything happening around me? I hope you are not in one of the operating offices spying on me?"

"I told you I am the Wizard of Oz."

"You are right," Maneta responded.

"Now baby, tell me, how does one go to your place?"

"Don't you know, Mr. Wizard? So, after all, there are many things you don't know."

They chatted for another hour, mostly bordering on the romantic. Wiz displayed many more pictures of himself. Each photo mesmerized Maneta more than the previous ones. How lucky she was, she thought, that she should not only have met a friend residing in the country of her dreams, but a man who more than fitted her desire. Luckier was she even more that she had met a friend who was eager to chat with her anytime; a friend who was not interested in asking for photos of her nudity. After about three hours on the Internet she signed off. Instantly, the attendant dashed to Maneta's desk and mocked her about the expiration of her thirty minutes.

Thirty minutes? Was this attendant really stupid, or was he away all this while?

She was shocked when the attendant even commended her for using the computer for exactly thirty minutes. In shock, but also lost in her memory of the company she had kept with Wiz, she advised herself to merely ignore the buffoonery and hasten out of the café.

At the exit of the café she caught sight of a lady jumping around in an excited mood. She remembered her as a fellow patron at the café, although they had never made an acquaintance. Smiling to herself, Maneta soon realized that the lady must have just gotten some good news. As she exited the door, she felt warm hands tapping her shoulder. She turned and held the beaming face of the cheerful lady.

"I have got it, the ticket and the visa! I am going to America!" The lady screamed.

By this time, three other ladies had joined her and they too were jubilating with her. Although Maneta was openly happy for her, yet she was baffled as to why the lady had brought her into the matter.

"Party time at the beach, and you are invited! We are off to the beach. Food and drinks are on me. My boyfriend has done it for me, and so I have to celebrate tonight."

Maneta was just about to thank her for the invitation, and to assure her that even though she would not be making it, she was truly happy for her, when the lady shoved her ticket and her passport into her hands.

"Take a look! There you will find the green design of the American visa!"

Maneta looked at it keenly. Was Wiz going to bring such happiness to her face? The jubilant lady held Maneta by the hand and pulled her into the taxi that had just been hollered at. The taxi took off at high speed leaving a cloud of dust behind it.

The nightclub was already crowded by the time Maneta and the other ladies arrived. The air was full of the stench of cigarette smoke and the music was at high volume. The dance floor sweated with the perspiration of the dancers. There were jubilations and congratulations followed by several snapshots. One girl walked up to Maneta, and without the formalities of a new acquaintance brought out a picture from her handbag and showed it to her.

"Do you think this is a nice picture to send to my

boyfriend?" the girl enquired.

Maneta looked at it closely as if she were scrutinizing it for faults. "But you wouldn't send this picture with someone to give to your boyfriend. It will quickly pass around from one hand to another, and people will see all of that body of yours."

"No, I'm not giving it to anyone. I'm in-boxing it to my boyfriend's Facebook message—for his eyes only. Nannette sent many of these to her guy before the ticket came running for her to go to the USA." The girl said, returning the picture to her bag. "If they don't see they don't buy. People here don't know good things. He is a white guy. His dad worked here many years ago as a Peace Corp. He said he would be glad to take a wife from here." She took out the picture of the white man. "Lookie! lookie! We became Facebook friends some three months ago, and already he is paying my rents. He lives in Manhattan, New York."

Manhattan! Maneta's heart missed a beat. She quickly looked at the white man's picture again before she concluded that it was not her Wiz. Should she really send this kind of picture to Wiz Hardy. She had done it before, but it did not yield her any dividend; in fact, the Indonesian fellow did not even get back to her. Then she suddenly remembered that Wiz had commented, rather disdainfully, about her having too many pictures on Facebook. But before she became deeply lost in thought, the jubilating lady pulled her by the hand unto the dance floor.

It was past midnight when Maneta arrived home. Her apartment's compound was quiet and dark when she stepped into it. She stole her way through the rugged surface. Her daughter should be fast asleep at her neighbor's. She decided that she should let her alone and pick her up in the morning. Her neighbor wouldn't mind. She was sure of that. She therefore went directly to her door, but just as she was turning her key, her neighbor's door flew open.

"Maneta, I did not want this to wait until tomorrow," the neighbor said.

Maneta stopped fidgeting with her key. "I didn't want to wake you up only to collect my baby. I thought it was best to wait till morning. Hope she didn't cause you much trouble?"

The neighbor moved closer since it was dark and the two couldn't make out each other from the distance. Maneta noticed that she carried something in her hands.

"Is she still asleep?"

"This is not your baby. I received this package on your behalf this evening," her neighbor said.

"A package! From where?"

"How do I know? I wish I could read like you. The world's most handsome man brought it for you."

"Did he say his name?"

"He didn't say a word. He gave me a pen to sign, and when I told him I couldn't read and write, he produced a soft pad and I dipped my thumb and pressed it on his book. He gave me the parcel and left—it was more like he disappeared. His eyes were something else. They left me cold and weak," she chuckled and laughed. "Don't allow me to bore you. You must be tired and would want to know what you have in that parcel. Don't worry about your daughter; you can pick her up in the morning. She is sound asleep."

All tiredness had gone from Maneta. Her eyes were now

excited to discover what was in the parcel. When she entered her apartment she reached for the hurricane lamp and lit it. She returned to her parcel. It had come from the USA! And indeed her eyes were beholding the name of Wiz Hardy. She quickly tore open the parcel, and there surfaced a beautiful Dell laptop. Her heart missed a beat, another beat, and another beat. Her breath paused. She fell back on her chair. It was then that an exuberant excitement overwhelmed her and she burst out with the greatest happiness she had ever experienced. She returned to the parcel and discovered that other equipment were enclosed. There was a mobile modem to access the Internet. There was a spare battery for the laptop. A short note was tacked to the cover of the laptop. *This is to make your dream come true. That obnoxious Internet café attendant will never see you again. Enjoy your toy.* Signed, Wiz-Hard!

After fidgeting with the parcel for a while, Maneta dashed to her room. While in her room she was sure that she heard the rustling of the packet that was wrapped around the laptop. She carefully picked her steps to the door. She peeped. There on the floor, playing with the torn packet was her daughter. How could her neighbor just drop her daughter off after she had promised to keep her until daybreak? What was the meaning of this? The baby looked at her and laughed. She picked her up and kissed her, and told her not to mind aunty. She was probably dashing off to attend to a matter that couldn't just wait. She reached for the front door, but discovered to her utter surprise, that the door remained as neatly closed with the key as she had locked it on entering.

She fainted!

A blue glow appeared in the center of the laptop and after a while it began to increase in size. Maneta's daughter, who had sat crying after her mother had fainted, became attracted to the glow. She slowly moved toward the laptop. Meanwhile the glow kept increasing in size and its brightness took over the room. By the time Maneta's daughter reached the laptop, the glow had brightened to the point of spreading rays through the eaves of the door to the darkness outside.

In a while, a soft jingle began to play; the screen began changing into many other colors, ebbing and flowing like a sea. Three big bubbles appeared on the screen, rolling about. Maneta's daughter put out her left hand, attempting to capture one of the bubbles. She was enjoying the attempts as the bubbles kept eluding her fingers. She then thrust both hands at the screen. In that instant, the bubbles disappeared. The jingle stopped. The glow receded. Maneta's daughter's hands remained glued to the screen; she cried, unable to detach her hands. Then her hand sank into the screen, then her head, and eventually her entire body.

In that instant, Maneta gained consciousness. She just witnessed the laptop shutting up and the glow disappearing, leaving a dark screen. She felt an excruciating migraine, but she managed to stagger on her legs, screaming as she dashed for the door. However, before she could reach the door, the glow appeared in its full force, and divided into two ropes of flames, wrapping around Maneta's sides. Meanwhile, Maneta had succeeded in opening the door. She fought hard to free herself from the grips of the flaming ropes. The ropes themselves began to throw her from one side of the room to the other until she too was eventually swallowed into the laptop's screen.

Maneta felt her body floating in dark air. She felt the chilly sensation of being suspended. Then she experienced being lowered gradually until her feet touched the ground. The atmosphere was rather foggy just as her mind was.

As soon as her feet touched the ground a door appeared before her. She walked through it without knowing where she was going. Bright lights appeared that took away the fog from her eyes. She kept running into doors as though someone was after her. By this time she had run into three doors ahead of her, each leading to nowhere. Then suddenly, the ground gave way from under her and she fell through a wide abyss into a dark room. She remained still in the dark. Before long a blue glow appeared in the center of the room and began to increase in size.

The room became fully bright and Maneta was able to decipher the image of a hanging human being. She soon realized that it was her daughter. Mechanically, she screamed and dashed for her, but each time she forced her way towards her, the glowing light would pull her back. However, she kept assuring her daughter that she was going to be okay.

"We do not want your child, and we do not intend to hurt her if only you can stop screaming and listen to what I have to communicate to you," a voice said to her.

She could not place any face to it. "Whoever you are, why are you doing this to me and my daughter? Let her go, let her go, please. Don't hurt her."

"Very well, Maneta," The figure behind the voice appeared before her.

"Wiz Hardy!"

"*Ah, ah*, Wizard, not Wiz Hardy. Did you have a good trip to my USA? Follow me, Maneta."

Wiz automatically turned around and began walking through a door. As he moved, Maneta's hanging daughter began to follow him in the air. It was then that Maneta got up and followed after them. She increased her speed and tried to grab her daughter from the air.

"I wouldn't do that. Your daughter is hanging on a slim invisible thread—the thread of her own life. If you as much as touch her, the thread would cut and she would die."

They came to a big open place. A flat elevated alter was burning bright with candles on all four sides of it. Wiz turned to Maneta and invited her to sit with him at table. He informed her that she was in Virtual Land, a land that had been invaded by people of her kind. And since her kind was now more connected with each other on Virtual Land, war had to be declared over mankind.

"But Wiz, you are yourself human—you look like me and I look like you. Look how handsome you are. Why can't we all just live as one?" Maneta tried to reason.

"That's the problem with you humankinds. You think that anyone wearing this frame is a human. This is exactly why you humans are limited in everything: in wisdom, in capacity and in lifespan. Your frame is a prison. I am in this frame only because I am here to engage you. Remember when I had to show you a photograph of myself on Facebook? It was to help you control your thoughts of what I might look like, but I do not necessarily look like the fellow you are seeing right now."

"What do you mean by that? Is this not you that I am seeing right now?" Maneta asked.

"That's as much as you can see of me for as long as you remain to be only a human being. But there are many sides of me, and that's the wonderful thing about being a Virtualite. In addition to what we are and unlike you human beings we do not die."

"Why then are you threatened by us human beings? You have the ability to live forever. You are vampires."

"We are not vampires—even they are limited just like you are," Wiz said.

"In that case, every living organism has to have a limitation. You Virtualites have to have your own limitations."

At this point a protean anger boiled inside of Wiz. Maneta's reasoning hurt him so badly that he had to yell a big and long '*No!*' at her. He reasoned with her that only living beings that do not have the potential to be divisible could speak of limitations. He was still speaking angrily when he told her that he was going to demonstrate the Virtualite's power of being divisible, even as a single entity. Immediately, a gushing wind, coming from nowhere, began to spin around them at a high speed.

After the strange wind had spiraled around Wiz for a few minutes, his human form began to detach from his main frame: the head detached from the neck and hung itself just above the main frame. It was still communicating with Maneta. Then the hands detached and hung in the air considerably away from the body. The legs swept themselves from under and joined the hands. The torso began rotating in the whirlwind. While this was going on, Wiz assured Maneta that because he did not originally exist as a human body, all she was seeing at that moment was for her to understand what he meant by virtual divisibility. He then went ahead and changed each of the human forms into something else. Among the changes there appeared a big rock, a sea fish and a tree. Still engaging Maneta, he asked her to think of any object that she wanted him to change into. Maneta was unwilling at first, but after being urged, named as many as ten objects into which Wiz changed before he returned to his human form. The wind died down immediately after that.

At that same instant, Maneta's daughter slowly descended to the ground. Maneta grabbed her and began to run away. She ran back through the doors that she had entered. But wherever she ran, Wiz appeared in front of her. She began pleading with him not to harm them. She saw an opening on her right, and as Wiz surged forward to seize her, she escaped into the opening. It was a rather long opening. She and her daughter rolled on a long ride before being deposited on a heap of rubbish. Grabbing her daughter, she quickly took to her heels. Although she didn't know where she was running, she kept running very fast, as long as she got away from Wiz.

But soon a familiar voice began to call her name. She decided to risk stopping to enquire who it was. To her amazement, it was Abibu. *How could he have got here?* She wondered whether to trust him or not and decided that in her current situation no one was to be trusted. She reached for a fat log nearby and took a confrontational posture as Abibu approached her.

"Abibu, stop there! Why are you here?"

But Abibu kept advancing.

"I need you to stop right there." She held firmly to her daughter.

Abibu stood still. "What is going on here, Maneta? How come I'm here in this place? I was in your room a few minutes ago, how come you and I are here?"

Maneta realized that Abibu was as confused as she was. She lowered the log and Abibu came up to her and held her in his arms. Maneta began to sob.

"Something is happening to us, I don't know what."

"This has to be some evil force. Don't worry, we are going to try to get out of here," Abibu assured her. "What is that thing in your room with the bright light that blinded me? After calling your phone and not receiving a response, I visited your place. The door was shut. It took a hammer to open it. Some force pulled me in and then there was this bluish bright light that blinded me and I became unconscious. When I gained consciousness, I found myself here," Abibu reported.

Maneta spared herself explaining the entire story of the laptop. "That's the same mysterious happening that landed me and my daughter here."

In that instant a loud sound came from behind them. They heard the sound of horse hooves approaching. Abibu grabbed Maneta's daughter as they all ran into hiding. The noise grew louder and louder. From their hiding they were able to see the procession of Virtualites passing by. They all had on heavy armored dresses and straight faces as they marched along.

"That's the entire population in the entire existence of people of the Virtual Land," a voice came from behind them.

Maneta and Abibu swiftly turned around and grabbed whatever they found and began to hit the man behind them.

All the time he kept pleading that he was not one of them; he was a human being. They stopped beating him.

"Momodu, the name's Momodu Cole. They have kept me here for two years now. I am of no use to them, that's why they don't go after me."

Maneta narrated her encounter with Wiz and all that he had told her about himself. She also told them how he changed into the many objects that came to her head.

"He lied to you when he told you that Virtualites don't have a limitation," Momodu said.

"Yeah, he told me that they were unlimited in everything," Maneta remembered.

"I don't know where Virtualites come from but the entire population is not more than ten thousand in number. Yes, they don't die, that's true, but something else is bothering them. They are never able to be you…I mean they have tried to impersonate us but they cannot. They will always be ten thousand in number, no more, no less, because they do not reproduce their kind."

"Why is that a problem? I don't care to live forever and don't have to reproduce my kind," Abibu said.

"That's true only if *we* humans did not exist," said Momodu.

"How's that?" Maneta asked.

"Well, for one thing we have invaded their space. All the millions of viewers on Facebook, twitter, Tagged, Bing and all those chat sites have made life miserable for the Virtualites."

Momodu stood up. "Follow me," he said.

The three of them walked out of their hiding place. Abibu took Maneta's daughter by the hand.

Casting his eyes about, Momodu said, "Look at this place,

see how miserable the atmosphere is. When I was swallowed last year, this place had life. Virtualites could be seen all over the place socializing. But look at it now," he paused. "Their lives are now haunted by six billion earth people.

He paused for a while and continued, "That explains why any earth woman could be brought here. They want to experiment with infusing their genes into the human system to see if that could bring about a new species with seventy percent virtual genes and thirty percent human genes. They reckon that when this new person is sent back to earth, and mates, a Virtualite child will be born."

Maneta and the others saw an object falling from the sky. As it descended on them, it changed midair into a human form. There stood Wiz before them clapping his hands.

"Momodu, you have done well. What a good lesson on the limitation of Virtualites. You got it right; we Virtualites are the creation of the internet age. Yes, we do not reproduce. But when you say we will always remain ten thousand in number, there you have told the biggest untruth," he paced around them in a circlular motion. "You see, the very things that create problems for you are the things you can use to solve the problems."

"But no one has created any problems for you and your kind, Maneta shouted.

Wiz ignored her. "Human beings believe that they are the center of creation. But the truth is that while you may be the center of your own universe, you fail to understand that there are thousands of other universes where you do not matter. Millions of you have taken the pleasure of washing your dirty linens on cyber space, where we Virtualites are in the center of creation. Our lives have become miserable because of your Facebooks, Handbooks, Footbooks and all those other chat rooms you have created.

"But you are only ten thousand in number and you cannot fight us who are six billion and counting…don't you get that!" Maneta shouted again.

"Oh yeah," Wiz immediately took offense. "Don't I get it? What don't I get? I have tried to impress it on your mind that Virtualites are superior to you mortals. What don't I get? That you and your kind are a suffering miserable lot who have to eat every day to survive? Who are just limited in those frames of yours?"

"We are reasonable beings. Where we come from we strive to live in peace with each other," Abibu jumped in. "If you have issues with us your authorities can simply contact our earth authorities, and everything can be worked out for everyone's good."

"Virtualites do not have singular authorities over us. We all think like leaders, and so whatever I do here is the same any other Virtualite would do. You people need authorities because you are primitive and uncivilized. Speaking of which, I have a surprise for you." He turned away from them and spoke in a foreign dialect, and then in English, "Earthman, come forward."

A man covered in armor from head to toe, walked from behind a wall and marched directly to Wiz. Wiz examined him for a while before passing a next command in the strange dialect. Instantly the armor began opening from the feet all the way up to expose a human being.

"What?! What is the meaning of this?" Maneta shouted. "What have you done to him?"

"You are not mistaken Maneta. You are certainly seeing a

superior version of the attendant at the café you used to visit to access the Internet," Wiz beamed with joy. "You can refer to him as Earthman. He is half Virtual, half Earth. He has a mission. He is our first experiment of future Earthmen who would help Virtualites reproduce. Earthman has been programmed to mate with you Maneta, and to reproduce the completely new Virtualites!"

"You are mad!" Maneta shouted.

Earthman, formerly known to Maneta as the café attendant, continued to stand still as stone.

"No, madness is for human beings," Wiz responded. "Sorry earth people this conversation is over. Earthman, you have the power, Maneta Bongay is your mate. Go after her and make us Virtual babies!" He uttered a broad echoing laugh as he took off into the air, changing into many objects before disappearing in the distance.

Earthman took two steps forward and demanded the hand of Maneta by stretching out his own hand. Momodu, who had been quiet for most of the exchange, stepped forward to bar the way. They eyed each other with hostility for a while before Earthman elbowed him. Momodu was flung into the air before he crashed in the nearby dump. Earthman continued to advance on Maneta, who by now was cupping her daughter to her chest. Abibu uttered something unintelligible and confronted Earthman, lending his whole weight against him. Earthman staggered three steps backward, before hitting Abibu and sending him sprawling on the ground. Abibu and Momodu held tight fists as they both rushed at Earthman. Earthman reeled back from the blows and fell over in a heap. He quickly recovered and advanced on both men. He gave a solid kick to Abibu, again sending him rolling on his back. When Momodu took a stick and attempted to hit Earthman, he pulled an object from his right side and sprayed fire at him. Momodu cried aloud as he went crashing down and burning to death.

By now Maneta had grabbed her daughter and was running down a runway. Earthman followed her. Abibu also followed behind them. The chase took them from one alleyway to another. Earthman was spraying fire at every structure and blowing up anything in his way. Abibu was throwing objects at Earthman to distract him from Maneta and her daughter. When Abibu persisted with his throwing actions, this angered Earthman, who then turned his attention to Abibu. This gave Maneta and her daughter an opportunity to hide away. Abibu had also hidden himself.

Earthman turned around looking for him and slowed down at the end of one alleyway. Abibu who was holding a big net in his hand aimed for Earthman's head and dropped it on him. The net covered him all the way down to his feet. While he fought to remove it, Abibu shoved him and he tumbled over and rolled down the alleyway. Abibu then ran down to the other end to where Maneta had gone to hide. They quickly embraced. By the time they released each other, Maneta's daughter had disappeared. They broke off searching for her but none of the immediate locations yielded anything of her. Maneta began sobbing.

They quickly separated to search for her. Abibu suddenly stopped and looked keenly again before he shouted for Maneta to come over to him. Maneta quickly rushed over to where he was standing. Abibu pointed and Maneta followed the direction with her eyes. Below where they stood and in the middle of fire-gutted structures sat Earthman with

Maneta's daughter cupped in his hands. Maneta ran down the hill, pulling her hair and hurling threats of what she would do to Earthman if he did anything to her baby. Her threatening voice degenerated to crying. Abibu ran closely behind. When they reached Earthman they stopped.

Maneta negotiated, "Please, please don't hurt my baby…she is only just a baby."

Earthman's head was bowed and the little girl played and laughed.

"Baby you are going to be alright…just you hold on, Mama is going to get you from him."

"I don't think he means any harm to the baby, look, he is just giving her a gentle stroking."

"How can you say so? This thing just brought down this whole place and killed Momodu."

"I am not going to hurt your daughter, I am not."

"You see, I told you," Abibu took Maneta by the hand, pacifying her.

A few seconds passed before Earthman raised his head to look at Maneta and Abibu. Maneta did not remember ever beholding such a mangled and patched up figure. The only evidence that proved that she stood before the man she used to know as the attendant at the café she frequented was his face. Hesitantly, she moved closer and closer to him.

"Maneta, this is me, the guy who used to trouble you at the café. Look how miserable I am," he began to sob.

"It's going to be okay. Let's try to get out of here."

Maneta tried to help Earthman to his knees but the effort was futile. He requested Abibu to help, but the effort was still futile. Earthman continued to sob, seeking to know how much destruction he had caused under the spell of the

Virtualites. Maneta wanted him to control his emotions so she told him how much power he used to destroy huge giant buildings and how he had killed an innocent poor man who had only come to her aid

"You must restrain yourself from killing your fellow human beings and instead try to get us from this wretched situation," Maneta reasoned with him.

"Go!" Earthman uttered in one breath.

"Go?" Maneta questioned.

"Yes, go. The Virtualites are out searching for me. They are on their way here."

Maneta grabbed her baby and together with Abibu hid behind a thick wall.

"Don't you people go too far, I promise to rescue you and send you back to Earth.

From where Maneta was hiding she could see four Virtualites approach Earthman. They spoke to him, examined him and took him off in a stretcher. He had been badly wounded. Maneta and Abibu watched until the stretcher was out of sight. They sat on the floor, realizing for the first time, since the beginning of their ordeal, that they had not had any food or drink of any kind. Five minutes later they were sprawled on the floor, fast asleep.

Maneta felt a cold touch on her arm. She was startled from her sleep and opened her mouth to scream. Earthman immediately covered her mouth to stop her from screaming. He told them to follow him at once. Hesitantly they stole into the dark behind Earthman. Walking into endless darkness, Maneta and Abibu took turns at carrying the baby on their shoulders. When they came to a particular spot, Earthman shouted for them to stop a little away from him.

"I have been given more Virtualite genes in my system and unless we can send you off quickly I will turn against you and seek to destroy you. Do not waste any more time. Do as I tell you and you will be gone from this place. If I can escape from here I shall be coming to Earth soon—after all I am Earthman."

That little bit was meant as a joke to ease the tension, but there were no nerves left for fun in Maneta and Abibu. Earthman knelt down and opened a vault. It was an empty vault with only a bright bluish light.

"Now all of you get in here," Earthman ordered.

Maneta and Abibu hesitated.

"Trust me on this one—but that trust may not be for too long before I change to my Virtualite self."

First to go was Abibu, before Maneta, thanking Earthman, stepped into the vault with her daughter strapped to her back. Earthman looked at them and wished them good luck. But just as he was shutting the vault, he felt a spasm. He yelled into the thick black night as he broke off the lid, and stretched his hand to grab Maneta by the hair. He roared and roared and called on other Virtualites to stop the escape of Maneta and her daughter. Maneta and Abibu struggled to close the vault with the broken lid. They could hear more voices approaching. It was getting too late for them before the lid finally fitted and a gentle bust of flames swallowed the night and took off into the air.

Maneta, her daughter and Abibu materialized in her room. Dumbfounded, they searched around in disbelief. Everything in her room was as she recalled leaving it. The laptop still sat on the table, harmless and cold. Except for the door that had been broken in. How was she to tell this story? Who was going to believe anyway? Meanwhile her daughter cried for food.

"I think I should out and look for something to eat," Abibu offered.

"No, don't go, I should. Let me find out what people are saying," Maneta said.

She stepped out of the door. There were the usual noises of housemates cooking and doing other chores. At first nobody seemed to take any notice of her. She felt her body to confirm whether she was visible or not. She proceeded to a housemate whom she requested from and received a bowl of newly cooked rice. She quickly walked back to her room. Was it that nobody knew what she had gone through? She returned to the room only to meet Abibu staring at the laptop. He was so engrossed in it that he didn't hear her inviting him to have some food.

"You might want to take a look at this," Abibu said.

"That computer again! I need to get rid of it."

"Not so fast. Come and take a look at this," Abibu insisted.

"This is who you know as Earthman. I sent you this message before I let you into the vault. Please keep your laptop with you, I shall communicate with you anything I want you to know. But for now, please alert the authorities that the Virtualites are about to bring doom to earth."

That night while Abibu was sound asleep, Maneta took the laptop and dumped it in the toilet outside. Her life and that of her daughter couldn't be brought into this madness. She returned to sleep. Several days passed before she decided that her life and that of her child had returned to normal. She had no intention of going near any café just yet. That no one seemed to know anything about her ordeal made her believe that she, her daughter and Abibu would have been bewitched if it were not for the intervention of God. Church became her foremost preoccupation. The devil had to be cast out by all means.

After confessing in church that her previous life of greed and love of money had made her a target of the devil she had agreed with the congregation that only praying ceaselessly could bring back her stolen soul to the Lord. At night, lighted candles were her armor to keep the devil away. The Bible was always neatly laid under her pillow. She had only once removed it from there temporarily when it was obvious that she was going to make love to Abibu. Not that Abibu believed that he and Maneta had been bewitched, but he reasoned that it was best to follow in Maneta's line of thinking as a way of providing succor to her.

One night when it was not possible for Abibu to sleep over at her place because his wife needed extra help, Maneta sang all the joyful songs of redemption that she had learned, backing them with copious verses from the Bible. She went to sleep with the Bible under her head and three candles glowing in the center of the room. The laptop appeared before her and she went into a barrage of prayers to cast the devil off.

Earthman's message and the laptop stayed in the room: *unless Maneta reported the matter to the political and military authorities, earth was doomed.* That night Maneta took her daughter, boarded a taxi and went to the church building where the pastor gave her a place to spend the night. However, the night refused to pass uneventfully because Earthman wanted her to hear him out. She sought solace in the toilet, the laptop went after her, in the garage, the laptop went after her; finally in the vestry, the laptop went after her. Earthman reasoned out with her that if he were of the devil it would all have stopped. Maneta finally gave up. At dawn, she returned to her room where the computer was waiting for her, but this time it did not bother her. Following a lengthy cyber exchange, she agreed to approach the authorities? But which authorities? Certainly not her church authorities. She knew now that this was not a church matter.

However, after the police and the military had turned her down and after the media and the civil society organizations had turned her down, she returned to the church. The pastor agreed to spearhead her 'final days' campaign. She tried to tell the pastor that this was not a 'final days' campaign but a modern reality. The pastor gathered the congregation and they threw their weight behind her.

But by the time the media were picking the story from the church and publishing details of it for the political authorities to take action, the strange people were already among human beings. Before long, buildings were being blown up in central Freetown. The church became afraid of Maneta. Her pastor and his congregation quickly abandoned her, and in fact accused her of using the powers of Jezebel to cause mayhem. The media embraced her vehemently, articulating in detail anything she said that Earthman was telling her. Earthman wanted the Sierra Leone government to alert the American government to join forces in the fight against the Virtualites.

America and other countries ruled out any intervention into what they described as the country's civil war. The African Union and the Economic Community of West African States warned that they didn't have any more resources to help address a second war in Sierra Leone. Finally, Maneta had a message for America and all others who thought it was just a one country affair*: the Virtualites, numbered ten thousand immortals are now all over Africa and America.* Other African countries were reporting destructions with no enemies in sight. Every day the destruction was claiming the lives of citizens and property. No country could quell the destruction and the killing. Maneta became highly sought after: *What else was Earthman saying?*

The United States Government requested that since this war appeared to be a cyber space war, it would be helpful for Maneta to be where the technology to track down cyber communications was. Maneta and Earthman were suddenly the most important figures on Earth, as the world powers realized that with all their chemical and nuclear arsenals they couldn't defeat the Virtualites.

While at NASA headquarters, Maneta picked up another signal from Earthman: *The whole world should agree to shut down every computer and laptop for forty-five minutes.* In that period of time, the Virtualites, who were only immortal while in Virtual Land, and could not survive on Earth for thirty minutes if they couldn't find powered-on computers to infiltrate, would disappear forever.

The American president needed to give his consent to turn off all computers in America—but a certain General was on record saying "How can we allow a third-world sorcerer from Africa to instruct us on un-militaristic warfare? The whole of the civilized world is connected to the cyber world—Do Maneta and her Earthman know what that means?"

The world continued to look on as the death toll rose and the destructions continued. Then another American war general suggested that computers could be turned off regionally instead of all at once. The decision was accepted by war leaders but no advice was sought from Maneta and Earthman.

All of Africa and Asia turned off their computers. Two hours later the destruction continued. Reluctantly, the leaders of America, Russia, China and other world powers met following pressure from their citizens to heed Maneta's advice.

Finally, at midnight of the thirtieth day since the invasion by the Virtualites, all computers, laptops and artificial energy were turned off from one end of the world to the other. The world waited…

The destruction sustained for thirty minutes before everywhere went silent.

The world waited for another hour and when there was no longer any destruction, it was declared that the military of every country was to comb all areas as a last attempt to trap any remaining enemies. After three hours of that operation, all computers and energy operated machinery were allowed to be turned back on. The world had never suffered such human and material loss.

Speaking from NASA headquarters, the American president declared the world a winner over invaders from Cyber Space. He specifically wanted the world to identify Maneta as the hero. "As for us in America, we are awarding Maneta the highest military decoration in the land and an opportunity to become an American citizen!" The president said.

Receiving the award, Maneta cautioned "Now we all as human beings should know that we should not continue to be our own enemies. There could be too many enemies out there bent on eliminating us, and therefore our only option would be to stop all wars amongst ourselves today and unite against any future invasion," Maneta said. "When I go back to Freetown, Sierra Leone, I shall let my people know how much you Americans appreciate our effort in helping to save the Earth from external aggression. I dedicate this award to my daughter who bore it all from Earth to Virtual Land, Abibu, a personal friend, and one other person who may still be trapped in outer-earth."

In that instant, she beheld the face of Earthman in the crowd. His eyes glowed like those of Wiz Hardy. Her heart sank. She lost him in the crowd before the applause.

Arthur E.E. Smith

MR. DEMOCRATICUS BRITTANY JONES' HARD DAY AT HOME

Mr. Erasmus Democraticus Brittany Jones lay soundly asleep like a newly born babe, innocent and oblivious to the problems of the world to which it has been born. Mr. Democraticus Brittany Jones kept snoring hard while he lay on the soft comfort of his *Vono* mattress which he was jealously stuck to, seeming not to be harbouring the slightest intention of parting with its comforting company. And why should he when you remember that only the previous day, he had returned home dead tired after spending extra hours in the office going through a pile of files in preparation for the station's tour by the company's directors from Britain.

If you should just look out, you'd realize that the night is now pitch-dark, being well past mid-night. If also, you should look keenly enough through the density of trees and foliage out there you might just manage to sense the frolicking and rummaging animals who form the predominant constituent of neighbours for Mr. Brittany Jones.

Much earlier in the night if you were here with me, you would have heard the noise of cars speeding off to distant destinations intermingled with the serenading sounds of birds and the chirping of crickets. But for such sounds of nature and those of the animals, the vicinity remains serene. Few people venture out now so late in the night especially with the recent increasing reports of armed as well as highway robbery at this suburban end of town, which is the favoured reserve of the affluent and more important segment of Freetown society. Houses here as you could see are normally far apart as each is endowed with vast land fit for even cultivating a farm. In such settlement, with the nearest house being a far cry away, as you would expect, security could be of great concern. This has been the case for Mr. Democraticus Britanny Jones who has therefore armed himself with a day and night guard as well as three fierce Alsatian dogs. As an added precautionary step, Mr. Britanny Jones will, on a daily basis even when returning home stone-tired, go through the whole length and breadth of his wide compound along with the night watch and his dogs, armed with a long view flashlight. Finally, upon retiring into the house, he would check to ensure the doors and windows are securely shut before retiring to bed to recoup his strength for another day's work. Even though living at this end of town makes huge demands on his time and resources, Mr. Jones still prefers the solitude and tranquility of that suburban milieu which affords him better rest after a heavy day's work to the noisy agitations and hustling of mid-town.

So Mr. Democraticus Jones continues enjoying his tranquil rest in splendid comfort in a double walnut bed. Then all of a sudden, all that changes for unease as he starts shuffling and rolling from one side to the other. Almost at the same time the dogs burst into a frenzy of barking joined by a cacophony of crying and moaning from the forest. Mr. Jones' rolling and shuffling becomes more agitated and regular in its irregularity. He also starts moaning and all of a sudden drops down from the bed on the floor. Almost involuntarily he raises himself up and moves towards one end of the room. Now at the door post he lifts one hand and presses it against the wall. The room is lit.

Moving unsteadily as if drunk and almost falling, he moves out into another room, switches its light on and takes a close look. He rubs his hand over his eyes and looks through the room again. He didn't seem to believe what he was beholding. He couldn't believe that this was his parlour now in such a disorderly state as if he had had a party that night. Still not accepting the reality of what was presenting itself to his view, he took yet another careful look at the whole room carefully scanning and taking stock of all what has been disarranged and all what could not be seen. Still unready to accept what was being revealed to his startled eyes, he dashes back to his room and retires to the closet where he washes his face and rushes back to the parlour to verify the previous picture given of it. He takes another close look and could detect no difference from the original picture. He now concludes that someone has broken into the house and burgled him.

He then goes to the other three remaining rooms in quick succession. He examines each in turn. He notices with satisfaction that each one wears its normal look. One of them, the last one, was where his wife lay sleeping. He wanted to wake her up but remembering that she had not been feeling well lately, he decided against it. For he thought that the night's sleep would put her in good stead for another day. He bumps his head several times as he rushes back. He proceeds to the rear part of the house where he examines the main door. He finds it securely locked. So after opening it he jogs down the back stairs after putting on the security light which illuminates the vast expanse of the courtyard. He heads directly towards the garage where the two vehicles are supposed to be parked. He unlocks the door and after putting on the light and after assuring himself of their safety, and examining it, switches the light off and closes the door securely once again. He moves all around the courtyard examining even the walls and the gates but finds nothing unusual. Now standing in one vantage spot in this whole expanse of a courtyard, Mr. Jones as master of that property gazes in wonder and amazement at the vastness but yet well-secured and protected property whose walls are twelve feet high and whose wide and expansive steel gates make an almost impregnable suburban fortress.

Then suddenly infuriated at the thought that throughout this exercise no sign was seen of the night watch even amidst such noise of the dogs barking, he charges forward taking a quick march towards an outhouse at the far back end of the compound and stops abruptly in front of it.

"Open this door!" he explodes all at once. "Open this door, I say," he repeats and then peers through the keyhole on the door and waits for the likely response from within. But getting none, he snarls, "Amadu, open this damn door!" He paces around for a while giving some time again for any possible response from within, but getting pregnant with anger and desperation.

Having waited for a reasonable time without seeing any reaction, he upraises his head and flashing another look at the locked door, he moves outwards first, and then sharply turning around, he looks towards the offending room. Then getting further irritated he charges rapidly towards it and abruptly halting just a few feet away from it, raising another military-like cry.

"Amadu! Amadu! I SAY OPEN THIS DAMN DOOR RIGHT NOW!" He waits endlessly again in anticipation of some response but none again seems forthcoming. "This complacence really beats me," he grouses and then lays bare on the offending door a volley of bangs which sets it vibrating in response resounding through the walls. Still yet there is no reaction from within. Giving another volley of bangs on the poor door, he shouts out sharply again, "Open this damn door you damn stupid Amadu or I'll . . . . " Mr. Jones was rushing back towards the other end of the compound when he was halted by his wife asking him, "What's the trouble Democraticus? What is all this noise about?"

"Oh you were asleep all this while that's why you would not know. Just go back to the house and take a look at the parlour and you will appreciate what all the noise is about"

As Mrs. Jones retires upstairs to go and verify her husband's report as to what happened, Mr. Jones picks up a metal rod lying just beside their garage. He returns with it to the offending door and starts pummeling it as if to bring it down this time round.

"How did it happen, Democraticus?" asks his wife on her return to him.

"God alone knows," Democraticus replies about to strike again at the poor door. "No door or window broke or opened. Mysterious!" He gives a few more strikes at the door.

"Democraticus, I hope this man has not died inside that room," Mrs. Jones was only thinking aloud about a grim possibility. But that thought emasculates her husband for a while as he immediately drops the implement to face his wife squarely. He keeps looking at her for quite a while before he asks quietly, "Do you really think he might have died in there, Darling?"

"How else could one explain such reticence, Democraticus? You have been hitting this door for so long making such a hell of a noise that I'm sure would have moved any living being. As far as I was from here, the noise was heavy enough to have woken me up and made me unable to continue to sleep any more. I can't conceive of how any living being could stay in there and endure such noise reverberating through every part of the room. No one could remain at ease under such a situation. That is why I strongly believe that if at all that boy is in there it must be in a state of death. So I think it does make sense to bring the door down so that we could remove his body before it rots and starts stinking all over the place."

"I don't want to think so, Margie," smoothly counters her husband. "He was not ill last night, so I see no reason why he should have died so suddenly like that without any warning or sign whatsoever. I just can't believe that."

"Don't say that, Democraticus--life is very uncertain. Anything could happen at any time without any warning or notice. A man could go to bed in the evening and sleep until the next day and eternally. That's why we must always say thanks every morning to the almighty for seeing us through to see yet another day. For we are not better than those who have gone before us."

"That's not the point Margie. Listen. What I'm telling you is this. That boy is not dead. Besides there is no sign of death here as yet. There was nothing the matter with him yesterday and none as well today. It's just that he might be up to some monkey tricks and he is not just prepared to face us yet. With such determination, any man could put up with any amount of inconvenience as long as that keeps him from giving in to that which he is holding out against."

"Well okay, if you should say so then allow me to try to rouse him up from whatever he might be up to." With that Mrs. Jones drew near the door and in a pleasant and cajoling voice called out to the one within. "Amadu, please, you don't want to die in that room, do you? So please get out from there and come get some fresh air before you get suffocated. Come on out, good Amadu, it's already daybreak. Stop being naughty, will you? You're no longer a child, you know. Behave like a man who's alive to his responsibilities. There is much work waiting to be done here."

"Has he answered as yet?" asks Mr. Jones rather impatiently but expectantly.

"Wait for me, be patient. It's little by little we'll succeed in getting him out not immediately. So just give me some time." She then moves to the back of the outhouse. She puts her mouth right by the small fissure in the metal window and whilst giving it a gentle tap starts calling on him once again to respond. "Come on Amadu! It's high time you woke up. Every living being is now up and doing something productive and useful." Here she pauses and listens for any sign of his reaction. Not able to get any, she begins beating the window but not with as much force as her husband did the door. She goes on doing this until she gets tired and fed up with the routine. So she returns to her husband waiting at the door already armed with a heavier implement.

With one haughty look at his wife and moving swiftly towards the door, Mr. Jones retorts rather tauntingly, "Now let me see whether this would not be enough to wake him up from the dead." So with an equal degree of determination he starts applying the heavier implement on the door. This time it seems as if the whole building was being brought down.

The ground below where Margie Jones is standing is shaking like a volcanic eruption. If you were to have been there yourself you would have experienced even your very heart palpitating as hers was. Then somewhat instinctively, he stops and turns towards his wife in contemplative silence.

"What's it?" she asks visibly startled at his sudden break in rhythm.

'Just that it suddenly occurred to me that I heard a faint moan coming from inside there just now. But now to be doubly sure that my ears were not deceiving me, I'll give another series of strikes. I just want you to listen intently so as to verify the source of the moan or cry.'

Taking on a propulsive posture at an angle to the door, and lifting the heavy implement in readiness for another round of blows, he asks the waiting wife, "Are you ready? Get set. All right let's go" and with his wife alert and keenly listening, he propels three successive blows on the already battered door. Then turning to her anxiously, he asks, "Did you hear anything at all?"

"Yes I did," she quickly affirms. "It came from in there all right."

"Well, see how much progress we have made," he says with a mischievous smile lighting his formerly morose face. Then tensing it all up and picking the heavy crowbar, he announces with a flourish, "Now for the final showdown."

"Please, please Democraticus don't" she pleads in a rather cajoling voice.

"Don't what?"

"Please Eddie, please don't bring the room down on him. Please don't do that for God's sake."

"But when did I tell you that's what I am going to do? What I am going to do is to bring the door and not the room or building down, mind you."

"However, avoid further violence," she maintained.

"How else do you expect me to get him out in the face of such stubborn defiance and neglect?"

"Well you just leave this now with me and just look on," Mrs. Jones says as she takes away and puts aside the heavy implement. Then going towards the door and knocking gently on it, she calls out cajolingly, "Come on now, Amadu, come on out and let's talk for a while. Do you hear me, Amadu? Come out and let's talk things out once and for all."

"Eddie he's coming out now at last," she whispers intimately into Mr. Jones' ears. "But please don't scare him off more than you have already. Just listen to what he has to say."

A complete hush ensues as the door is being slowly dragged open, A sourly faced man of about thirty years of age emerges from behind the door, with hot steamy air following him out of captivity. He takes an initial survey of those he has to contend with and seeing Mrs. Jones' face seeming to be much more accommodating he starts the motions of greeting, "Morning Ma! Er... er...er... Morning Sir." He says ending up trembling like a leaf in contemplating Mr. Jones' grave demeanour. Mr. Jones burst out with long suppressed anger, loudly, "To hell with your morning!"

Amadu shaking with extreme fright stealthily shifts his position well away from his reach.

"What uselessness is this? It's totally hopeless,". "With all such hell of a knocking and shouting who could believe a living being who has not been declared insane would stay still inside amidst all the noise."

"Pa let me tell you some . . ."

"I don't want to hear anything from you . . . ."

"Democraticus please leave this boy with me. Don't keep worrying yourself until you end up bursting a blood vessel. I am really interested in what he has to say to explain this strange behaviour. It is true that he has behaved very badly. Whatever the situation might have been he should have answered when the door was being knocked. Surely I felt and could even have sworn no one living was in there."

"But Mamy just you try to listen to me. It is then that you would begin to understand what I have been going through. If I should tell you how I was feeling you would not tend to believe me now. But in reality though I was not dead I wonder whether that was not what one could call death. I was feeling as if my whole body was going away from me and I had entered another world. My ears were drumming with the sounds of insects abusing my eardrums. They seemed countless and stubborn. To God, Mammy Jones it is only just now that I started hearing what was going on around me. Then I heard you calling me. Apart from that I could hear nothing else."

'Do you really expect me to believe that? You mean that in spite of all the noise your master kept making here you didn't hear a thing? Even as far as I was from here I was rudely woken up from my slumber. Look my friend, please tell me another story.'

"Well you see Mammy that is exactly what I was saying that you won't believe. But Mammy let me swear that this is the whole truth"

Karamoh Kabba

THE RING

A woman lay still in bed after her morning chores. Heavy metal gates crashed, sending deafening shock-waves into her ear canal.

'Ah, he's gone,' she whispered as she climbed down from the bed.

She paced the length of the large bedroom on the second floor. Afterwards, she staggered down the stairway into the kitchen for a cup of coffee. As she climbed back up the stairs, she stared fixedly into the cup to prevent the coffee from spilling on the spotless floor.

On the third floor balcony of the house with a barbed wire-garnished-concrete-fence, she carefully placed the cup on a cocktail stool next to a luxurious sofa and flung her entire weight back into the sofa. She sighed, reached for the cup and took a few sips. She placed the cup back, crossed her legs and reclined into the sofa. Then, she pressed her thumbs against her temples tightly, pushed her hands backward over her ponytail, and flung her neck back as she heaved another sigh. Her eyes were now fixed on the scenic sea view on the distant horizon, away from the clusters of shanty houses below the fence, on the bank of the ocean.

Dawn was broken by the rising sun from under the calm sea. Bothered by the rays, she looked down and flinched at the brightened blot on the landscape below. So, she rose up, turned round and saw Marie coming from the stairways behind her. Both women avoided the blinding rays and blemished seafront until twilight when the woman would return for an evening dose of the scenic sea view before Mojo returned home.

Marie was a next-door neighbour who visited the woman after their husbands left for work. Now, the two women walked into the parlour where they indulged in their usual conversation; this was the only way they spent their time barred behind their social gates.

The evening birds had flapped their wings away, and disappeared into the distant horizon. Freetown's raucous noise from *okadas*[5], *podapodas*[6], taxis and peddlers, just a short distant north, had hushed down earlier than usual. The evening winds blew heavier than predicted, fomenting into small twisters below faster than accustomed to, on the sea front. Overhanging dark and vapour-laden clouds suppressed the emergence of the evening stars. Bright lights from speedboats that jet in and out of the lagoon had also disappeared into anchors and docks along the seafront. Blinded by dust particles, the woman rose up from the sofa that evening and docked into the large bedroom.

The woman lay on her back. She crossed her fingers under her ponytail and dropped her elbows against the headboard. Like on many other nights as this one, she took pleasure in looking up at the creatively carved-out pretty red-wood patterns on the ceiling. Jaded, she reached for the bedside cabinet and took out a movie disc from the top drawer.

---

[5] Okada is probably of Nigerian origin; small motorbikes used as means of public transportation in Sierra Leone since after the decade-long civil war.
[6] In Sierra Leone Krio lingua franca, *podapoda* is usually a van used for public transportation.

The label read: *A Walk in the Clouds*[7]. The woman had seen every title in her collection but that one. She wondered how she possessed the new title. Puzzled by the fact that Mojo had no interest in movies, she knew it could not have been a gift from him. *Even if Mojo, who had stopped being romantic long ago, wanted to give me a gift, it wouldn't be a movie,* she convinced herself.

The woman had spent two weeks with her parents in a village called Bumpe, a fortnight ago. She tossed the idea in her head that; *during her absence, Mojo had invited a mistress over who must have forgotten the disc in the room.* But she however conditioned her mind to refrain from thinking thus, afraid that her thought might be misunderstood by Mojo, leading to needless ranting and raving from him. So, she resigned herself to a fate of silence.

The woman's dream of going to America had been further roused, over the years, by Hollywood movies. She rose up, popped the disc into the player and reclined back into the pillows against the headboard.

As the story progressed, she developed a bizarre interest in the stark contrast between the manner she had been offered into marriage by her parents many years ago and the way the young and handsome man wooed the beautiful character in the film. She took a deep breath, wiped her blurred eyes and slept off what ended up being an additional distress.

But between the sobs, the woman had relapsed into her usual imaginations of fond expectations of life in the US where she hoped to live a better life with her fantasy man:

---

[7] A Walk in the Clouds (1995), a film directed by Alfonso Arau. With Keanu Reeves, Aitana Sanchez-Gijon, Anthony Quin, Giancarlo Giannini.

An imagination of a young college student she wished to start life with was awakened: How they would stroll up and down Mountain Top College to spend weekends together in the university campus; how they would struggle together without a gated home or a big car slammed at her face; how in the rainy seasons, vehicles would drive past them and splash muddy water over them and how they would laugh it off happily; how they would play down at the creek, where she would run into the small stream between boulders and jagged-edges, lift her skirt up to provoke passion, after which, the man would run after her the rest of the way into his dormitory. And she would have no qualms.

She just could not understand why her parents deprived her of that kind of love for a life full of boredom in a gated property.

The woman's hope of life in the United States with her fantasy man came true in a long winded but twisted dream that night:

"'My left leg is numb,' she moaned.

The man massaged it with Deep Heat Ointment, but the numbness reigned. The woman reached for the glass of water she always placed on the lamp-stand every evening before she went to bed and gulped a painkiller and a muscle relaxant.

'Do you have a chest pain?' The man asked.

'No!' she answered.

'Do you have pain in your left upper arm?' The man continued.

'What about in your legs?' He insisted.

Now, the woman was eerie, 'No, I have pain nowhere in my

Leoneanthology

body. Leave me alone!' She snapped.

'You probably need to check into the hospital then,' he shrugged.

The woman groped for the receiver in the semi-darkness to place a call.

'Hello,' she paused….I have this strange coldness in my leg Doc,' she paused again. My husband suggested that I check into the emergency room,' she listened. It's been like this every night for the last three nights,' she waited. I am very worried now Doc,' she stated firmly.

Intermittently, she muttered: 'Hmmm …, nope..., not really...'

And then, she placed the receiver between her neck and her right shoulder, reached back to undo her ponytail as she listened for a while, and suddenly; 'Oh *reallyyyy*!' She almost shouted. 'Thanks Doc. I feel better now,' she said and hung up the phone.

She turned away from the man, cuddled a pillow and wept.

'What did he say to you?' The man asked nervously.

The man had felt better when he heard the woman telling the doctor that she felt better now. But puzzled by her renewed petulance, he sat quietly in the bed.

On one of the four quadrants of the room between light and the man, like The Thinker[8], was a gloomy silhouette of him. Gazing at the shadow of the man, she mumbled in great despair, 'He said I am suffering from depression,' as though she was talking to the shadow on the wall.

---

[8] In reference to the great French sculptor, Auguste Rodin's (1840 – 1817) 'The Thinker' (1880), especially in reverence of its sitting position as reflective of one in deep thoughts.

Troubled, the once slender young student of the woman's imaginations hustled his heavy weight away with enormous effort into the children's room for a good night's rest.

Although the woman was not visibly overweight, she however flung her weight thudding into the couch and ran out of breath. This breathlessness only happened walking up the entire stairs leading to their fourth-floor apartment.

In the morning, she went into the bathroom. Once in front of the mirror, she watched herself with great despair. She flinched, only to beam on a neat display of empty containers of brand name products that lined the sink, well-organized as in a personal hygiene aisle. She frowned, pulled the shower curtains apart, and revealed two half-empty tubes of generic shampoo and conditioner in the tub.

The man was in the kitchen with the kids, arguing with them about 'what's for breakfast'. Usually, he would have woken up earlier than he did to take the children to school on time for breakfast in school.

There was no milk in the refrigerator to prepare cereal for them. There was only one egg left. He was relieved that there was enough pancake mix, a feeling that only lasted till he realized that the pancake syrup too had finished to the last drop. At that, he felt a surge of lameness run through his body.

The woman came out of the shower just in time. The kids were rushing to her, hugging and shouting; '*mommmmyyy*,' one after the other.

The thought of no food in the house caused a pang in her chest.

'Where is your dad?' she asked.

'We don't know,' cried the youngest child.

'He left to go somewhere,' mumbled the other as he rubbed his stomach.

'He went to buy syrup,' the third explained.

The woman led the children back into the kitchen. She looked anxiously for syrup to spread over the three plates of pancakes the man had lined up on the dining table. Frenziedly, she removed empty food boxes from the refrigerator and shoved them into the garbage bin. Quickly, she knotted the trash bag and removed it from the bin. She set the bag full of trash aside to look for a fresh trash bag to reline the empty bin only to realize that the trash bags were finished and she had knotted the filled trash bag along with the empty box.

She turned round and saw the empty bottle of syrup on the far corner of the countertop, just where the man had left it before he dashed out of the apartment to buy another one.

The refrigerator door was still only ajar as the woman dropped her lame body against it. She pulled her weight up slowly, with a distorting look and tightly clenched fists. She jabbed repeated blows on the refrigerator, sending the kids, who had queued behind her, in great expectation, away on each other's heels in fear.

Exhausted from the jabbing, sobbed profusely before she turned around to behold the eyes of the man, who had returned from the store with a bottle of syrup, and was standing still and watching her in bewilderment.

The woman was satisfied to see a new bottle of syrup, but in the mix of anger and mortification, she said nothing to the man when she walked by him back to the room to finish dressing for work.

In front of the dresser draped with dirty linens, she took a tube of lotion from under a pile of more dirty linens. She shook out every smidgen of it onto her palm and rubbed it sparingly over her body.

The woman returned home from work that evening took a quick shower and dashed out to pick Joe and June up from school. Only then, the man left for work, just what they had to do since they could no longer afford a baby-sitter for Sarah.

Joe and June tossed their school bags, shoes and clothes everywhere in the apartment, from where they picked them up to go to school the next morning.

The woman then headed for the couch by the door to recuperate from shortness of breath from walking up and down the stairs, before she went into the kitchen.

From the refrigerator, she took out a bowl of rice and soup she had cooked a couple of days ago, threw it into the microwave, dished it into three separate smaller bowls and lined them up on the dining table alongside three glasses of water. Back in the living room, she returned to the couch. She heard some roughening sound on the doorknob. She opened the door just when the footfalls of the unexpected visitor faded away into the long corridor. On the doorknob was a piece of paper; the sheriff had delivered a non-payment of rent citation. She removed it quickly from the doorknob to prevent her next-door neighbours from seeing it, to avoid embarrassment. Then, she returned to see how the kids were doing on the dining table.

Today, Joe, the oldest of them ate much of his food. He seemed to be more understanding. June and Sarah complained when the woman asked as to why they had not touched their food.

'There is nothing to eat mommy,' June replied.

'But I just gave you food,' the woman retorted.

'Rice! Rice! And rice! Every day!' June and Sarah fired back at once but petulantly.

The woman walked away and returned with the man's leather belt, neatly wrapped around her clenched fist:

'Start eating now!' she threatened. 'Now, I say!' she smacked the belt against the dining table, before the terrified two ate clumsily.

Very irritated by the confrontation with the kids, she returned to the couch to watch her favourite afternoon talk-show in her quiet time. An episode struck a chord in her, and so she retired into a deep melancholy; how she could not afford the things she used to afford; about the late rent, interest rate and court fees; and many other unpleasant memories of hardship.

She recalled that only two years ago, they were spending three times less than now on cooking gas. Their groceries cost had doubled since then. Their other utility bills had almost doubled as well, but her salary had remained the same besides the twice fifty cents raise she had gotten since. She was more so saddened by the fact that the man, a cab driver, drove many more hours now and brought home a bit more earning, but still did not make much difference despite the long hours away from home.

The woman discerned these things separately, but had difficulty in consummating them into a big picture. She viewed the socio-political and economic news with great disinterest and was therefore far removed from the reality that the poor were getting poorer, the middle class was depleting and the rich were getting richer in the society she cherished in her real life. Doing her nails and watching talk-show after talk-show and being able to afford the basics without the prevailing hardship was consoling her despondent life in the couch a great deal until bed time. On her way home from work, she had stopped by the pharmacy and picked up her Prozac prescription. She pushed one down her throat that evening, feeling good and sedated, she slept soundly.

The woman was always asleep by the time the man returned home, but was always awakened by his noisy entrance. She snapped when he pulled off some little romantic tricks on her. Unmoved, she instantly accused him that he is only concerned about sex and not any meaningful relationship.

In anger, the man would leave her alone. They argued very late at night, rudely waking the kids from a premature sleep, who in turn went to school tired and sleepy.

Unable to cope, the man returned home. Now, left in much more difficulty of handling the bills on her income alone, the woman was finally evicted from the apartment.

Employed in Sierra Leone, where his degree and international exposure proved to be an invaluable asset, the man placed a call to the woman, 'You and the children can return home anytime you wish to do so....'"

... And the call was interrupted by the deafening ring-tone from the cell phone under the woman's pillow. She had set the alarm for 5:30 a.m. at which time she woke up to do her morning chores. The alarm had gone off and snoozed for a prolonged time and stopped, unable to wake her up from the protracted dream.

Mojo, who did not look forward to challenging the stairway back into the large room, once he was downstairs, had used his cell phone to call the woman instead, and his voice went thundering 'Hello, Wara! Wara!'

Too sleepy to recognize Mojo's voice, 'Hello, who is it?' the woman asked.

'Mojo!' he announced before he hung up.

Now fully awake, she realized that Mojo had been sitting downstairs in the dining room for at least thirty minutes waiting for his breakfast. She hurried out of bed, walked the short hallway between the large room and the stairway. Tired of waiting, Mojo too was struggling his way up the stairs with enormous effort, exerting every bit of energy a hungry obese man could muster. Halfway down the stairs, the woman was accosted by the massive frame of the big man of the house, the complete opposite of her fantasy man.

He enquired in a very angry inflexion, 'What's wrong with you today Wara?'

When she tried to force her way through without saying a word, Mojo slammed his heavy hand into her face, before he managed his frame back downstairs, causing lots of rumbling in the stairway as his boots went crashing on the marble tiles.

The woman was awakened to another rough start to that fateful day. Her wedding ring, the symbol of her love she had placed on his finger ruptured the lips he had kissed before God and man after the Pastor, many years ago had ordered, 'You may now kiss the bride.'

The woman cupped her hands under her face and collected dripping drains of blood and tears as she screamed for help.

Suddenly, she recalled that Marie had given her a telephone number for the FSU[9] two years back. But the thought of having to live a life just like those outside the gates below, flashed through her mind for a moment. She cherished the affluence within the walls of the fence as much as she hated the looming ill-fated destiny of a woman born in a family of poor subsistent farmers, whose parents' wish of offering her to a rich man in marriage had been guided by her own desire to live in wealth. But thoughts of the many years of abuse she had endured and the many more she would have to endure possessed her even more.

'Do it!' she whispered, as she buried her head between her thighs; wept and dialled the number Marie had given her.

---

[9] FSU (family Support Unit is Sierra Leone Police's responsible for intervention in domestic violence and other family related issues that require police intervention.

Kosonike Koso-Thomas

THE PINEAPPLE LINE

It is Friday, a trading day in the village of Masanta. Early morning light struggles to pierce the dark clouds gathering in the skies above. In the centre of the village, tradeswomen are hoisting baskets of fruits, vegetables and other goods unto their heads. The tradeswomen begin to move in small groups, ambling up a steep path towards their market stalls on the adjacent highway. Leading the first of these groups is Ekuma and Falala, her sister-in-law. They walk with unsure steps on the ruggedness of the path before them. Suddenly, a rumble coming from the direction of the old entrance into the village stops them.

"What's that sound? Could it be those rebel soldiers again?" Ekuma cries.

"Ay! Ay!" screams the last woman in the line. She drops her basket and runs into the bush.

Ekuma freezes.

The increasing rumble frightens Ekuma who begins to tremble. That noise. It drags her mind to the past: *The rumbling of light trucks, whining engines, gun shots cracking, red angry flames rising from thatched roofs, rape, and pillage.* Their fright is real; of men. Not just ordinary men. Wild red-eyed men steeped in the brutal intensity of violence.

A convoy of three 4x4 pickup trucks carrying unarmed foreigners and businessmen emerges and speeds out onto the highway and off towards Makata, raking dust into the air. Ekuma sighs in relief and calls out to her mates to continue their journey. She emerges from the brush, inhales the cool breeze blowing through the leaves that gave her and her group shelter and assures the group that it was safe to move on.

Arriving early at the highway is always rewarded with profit from quick sales to travellers heading westward to Frimanton, the capital city in the early morning hours. The volume of westward traffic swells, with trucks headed for markets at Luma and Wema, commercial centres on the outskirts of Frimanton. As the day wears on, the volume of the westward traffic decreases, while that in the opposite direction towards Makata increases. The women reach the highway and set up their stalls a few metres from the entrance to the village where a police check post straddles the highway lanes. In the area where the stalls stand, the road shoulder is eroded, exposing the compact layer of crushed rock beneath.

Selling at the stall always gives Ekuma a special bounce to her ego. She has worked hard to establish the longest and busiest stall on the "Line." The "Line" is the name the villagers have given to the highway; perhaps, because it stretches as far as the eye can see, in whichever direction one looks from Masanta. The "Line" is a new development which has resulted in considerable improvement to the old road and was completed only two years ago. Prior to its improvement, it followed a narrow and steep incline through thickly wooded hills before descending into the plains of nearby Rokang and meandering through the village of Masanta. Because of the steepness of this terrain and its slippery surface, local inhabitants named the hills "Slime Rock Hills."

The improvement avoids the hills, but also bypasses Masanta, killing business in the village which was once used as a stop over by drivers on long journeys. The police check post is a recent installation to stop the smuggling of minerals and arms into and out of the country. Masanta traders have revived their businesses by taking their markets to the highway. Travellers alighting from vehicles stopped by security officers for inspection are now their new customers.

Ekuma's business acumen has earned her respect among the village elders, but among women trading on the line, there is animosity. Some traders believe that she is trying to monopolize trade on the "Line". It is known that she buys her pineapples wholesale from farms in the village of Maposo, where the most delicious varieties are grown. Lashina Kador owns the largest of these farms and with him Ekuma has had a long standing arrangement to have the best of the crop of every year's harvest. Other traders often feel denied access to the better fruits. The Lashina-Ekuma arrangement now seems seriously undermined by Lashina's recent actions.

"I am worried about our pineapple supply we paid for from Lashina. There will be no fruit to sell next week," Ekuma speaks in a quiet but laboured tone.

"I thought Harouna, your brother has collected them already?" Falala says.

Ekuma remembers the many times she has had to put up with delays in getting her orders released by Lashina. Those disappointments have been upsetting and have often affected her business. The way Lashina treated Harouna, the last time he was at his farm to obtain pineapples Ekuma had paid for, shocked her. "This is outright advantage," she shouts, stanping her feet on the ground. A new pain erupts in her chest and it takes a moment for her to calm down.

Then she says, "No. He only allowed him to harvest a small quantity. Harouna is going there again in the afternoon to try and harvest more of what I am due."

Falala explodes with anger. "You have to show him that you are not a fool, Eku." She refers to her by the abbreviated form of her name, used often by her family and close friends.

"Certainly," she says. "If Lashina thinks that he can take my money and fail to deliver my pineapples, he is mistaken", Ekuma told Falala in a defiant tone.

"If Harouna does not get the rest from him today, I will go down to the farm myself and harvest the pineapples."

"I will come with you!" Falala declares.

"Thank you Falala, my sister."

"I know that Lashina's wife Ayie exercises subtle control over her husband's sale of the fruit from the farm. Getting the rest of your prepaid pineapples will be tricky, Eku! You need someone to help you get what is legitimately yours."

"We'll see. If the pineapples do not arrive in our house today we are going to move to Lashina's farm in the morning, Eku." Falala is clearly incensed by this wrong, and energised by her feeling against men who mistreat women. She remembers Anisa and Pepima in the village of Matolon where she grew up, who are neglected by their husbands after coercing them into bringing younger wives into their married homes. They now live in extreme misery.

"We may have to deal with Lashina's newest wife Ayie," remarked Falala.

"Why? I don't see how she comes into it," Ekuma replied.

"Don't you know, she is the one that determines pineapple prices and the quantity of the fruit that leaves the farm? I have this from reliable sources," she added. "Ayie gets her husband to sell only part of each day's harvest and retains the rest, which she sells privately at a higher price, to any trader who has not made deposits before the harvest,".

"What an awful conspiracy!" Ekuma says in disgust.

"That's what it is," Falala agrees. "If Lashina has taken money from buyers for today's harvest before Harouna gets to the farm today, there will be no pineapple to supply him, but he will have a quota for his wife to sell privately," she adds.

"So I should be a victim of their trickery, and pay more to Ayie for what she hoards?" Ekuma shouts. "No, not with me," she mumbles.

Ekuma's thoughts flash back to the days when she and Ayie were growing up in Monsoray. In Chief Alimamy's compound they lived like sisters. It was there, instilled into the children, that respect for one's self comes before respect from others could be earned. Both of them were initiated into the Bundo society the same year. In those days, they were taught not only the art of home making and craft skills, but also honesty and the virtues of hard work, decency and truthfulness.

"True," Ekuma replied. "But the moral of many of the stories we were told when we were young was that dishonesty doesn't pay. If you fail to learn from these morals at home, you will learn from experience in the streets," she said. "I have tried to follow the teachings of my parents and the community in which we grew up, and have not disappointed my parents so far," she adds.

"Where are your morals then, if you are planning to force your way into someone else's farm and seize his crops?" Falala asks.

"My conscience is clear about that," Ekuma says. Then she continues rather testily, "I have a right to go to that farm and get my money's worth of goods I have paid for, with money I sweated hard to save."

As the day draws closer to the evening, the line of vehicles travelling towards Makata begins to get longer at the check point. Passengers alight to permit inspection of their vehicles. Then, like a race, when the starting gun is fired, traders run from their stalls towards the passengers clutching fruit bunches and other produce, desperate to be the first to secure a sale. Then suddenly, light showers begin to fall. Ignoring the rain, they keep running towards the alighting passengers who are now scrambling to seek shelter. Some re-board their vehicles, a few others run towards the command post at the check point and there they are surrounded by a noisy crowd desperately trying to sell them everything they are carrying. Ekuma sees the rush of the other traders to meet the alighting passengers, but feels unperturbed. She has never joined the rush to get sales. She moves to the front of her stall and begins to cover the rows of fruits outside the area of the roof of the stall with sheets of transparent plastic.

"Falala, you go back home and get us umbrellas and some more plastic covering. I'll man the stall for now." She says.

"Why? This is mere drizzle. It will soon pass," Falala tells her, helping to cover the fruits.

"I don't think so. Get them anyway," Ekuma insists "We do not have enough here to cover the fruits," she explains and begins to remove those the sheets could not reach and puts them in baskets behind the stall. She then sits partly sheltered in the open sided stall. The rain begins to pour down heavier than before, hammering at the roof of the make-shift structures. Suddenly, a westerly wind begins to drive the rain at an angle which forces it through the front end of her poorly sheltered stall. For nearly ten minutes, it poured. She is trapped in her stall by the invading storm. Rain drops hit her forehead like pinpricks, then roll down her cheeks and disappear into the cleavage of her breast. Two mounds of flesh, stick out pointedly against the wetness of her white cotton bouba[10]. Falala has still not returned with the umbrellas and plastic sheets. Ekuma thinks of going back home and changing her clothes, but then the storm ceases and she sees a group of potential customers approaching her stall.

"Business before *yanga*[11]" she says to herself, and settles back into the hard plank on which she seats and waits for business.

Her clothes are now wet above her waistline where the folds of her lappa[12] hide the cash from her earlier sales. As customers reach her stall, she stands to attend to them. Then she notices a man dashing to join the line forming in front of her stall of pineapples. He pushes his way closer to view her fruit stand. The pineapples are golden yellow, mostly large in size and give out a scent of sweet freshness.

"Excuse me," he says to a lady in front of him and tries to push to the front of the stall.

---

[10] Bouba: Traditional ladies blouse
[11] Yanga: Beauty
[12] Lappa: A ladies tradition wrap (a traditional skirt)

"What are you doing?" She says. "You can't jump the queue. Our money is as good as yours," she continues, raising her voice.

"Reserve a basket of those for me, young lady," he yells over the head of lady in the front row.

"You mean you can come here and push regular customers like me out of the line and commandeer these pineapples. We who frequently pass through this Masanta checkpoint have known about these pineapples, and have patronized this stall for a long time" she says. "You just behave yourself and wait your turn."

The man waits till he can move to the front of the stall. He greets Ekuma and states his name. "I am Mordu Koka."

She acknowledges his greetings and smiles ready to sell more of her stock. With the rain slowly receding now, only the occasional spray of rain water reaches her where she stands. She puts on her trademark charm and comments on the weather.

"The rain is wreaking business today" she says and adds, "We should not have rain for another month; we cannot tell one season from the other."

"It's happening everywhere now," Mordu replies. "I work for the Hilltown Spring Water Bottling Factory. The weather pattern affects our business too."

Picking up two large pineapples from the display on her stall, he asks, "How much do I pay for these," his eyes fixed on the prominent trace of her breasts on her soggy *buba*.

She notices his gaze on her chest and feels a slight embarrassment, but says "Ten thousand for the pair".

Cursing under her breathe, she thinks, *Damn men, every little show of female bulge excites them.*

"I'll like to buy a lot more of these," he says. He has in mind the contribution he is expected to make towards the feast following the fortieth day funeral rites for his late father. "They will serve in place of mangoes which are now out of season," he reasons.

Ekuma dives into the baskets containing the pineapples she earlier removed from the front rows of her display and lays them out again on the stall for Mordu to select the ones he wants.

"Is it possible to taste one of these to assure me of their quality?" He says, not because he doubts the quality, but as an overture towards establishing friendship.

"Sure." Ekuma pulls out a knife and a plate from a basket under the display table. She peals and cuts one of the pineapples into neat slices. "Here you are, you can try these."

"Oh thank you." He takes a bite off one of the slices. "This is delicious; fresh, sweet and smooth. I'll take all you have. If all your pineapples taste as good as this, young woman, mark me down as a regular customer. I'll be back," he says as he pays for the pineapples.

"You are welcome," Ekuma says cheerfully.

"I am back this way on Sunday. Perhaps you will have more of these for me to take back to Hilltown," Mordu replies.

"Sure, there will be more on your return," she assures him.

Falala arrives with umbrellas and plastic sheets, just as Mordu leaves. "Why did you take so long to get just a few things?" Ekuma rebukes her. "What is there to cover now" she teases. "I have sold all the fruit while you were away and have to brave it out cold and wet while you were drying out at home."

She smiles, adding, "There was a man here while you were away who bought all we have in the stalls and promises to buy more on his return on Sunday."

"Lucky woman," Falala says. She hugs her and jumps around with her in a brief dance.

Ekuma's mobile telephone rings. It is Harouna. Ekuma answers. "I am back from Lashina's farm. He tells me there are no pineapples ripe enough for harvesting today," he tells her.

"Yeh!! Hear him. He thinks I can wait indefinitely for him to honour our agreement?" she tells Harouna. "Falala and I are moving into Lashina's farm in the morning to harvest the pineapples I paid for," she shouts with a determined voice.

In the dark grey dawn of Saturday, Ekuma and Falala set out on the five kilometre stretch of undulating gravel roadway to Lashina's farm. The surface is rough and sections of it are waterlogged from yesterday's heavy downpour of rain. Villagers have laid palm logs across the deeper pools of mud to raise the level of the road to allow vehicles and pedestrians to cross safely over the muddy stretch. They walk briskly along the side of the road. On either side are stretches of cultivated farms interspersed by thick forest bushes and wild palm trees. Several narrow accesses branch off the road into them and disappear into the creepy darkness. Now and again, trucks transporting firewood and charcoal from the forest speed past them..

Falala calls out, "I can't believe drivers can be so reckless with blind curves every one hundred metres!" moving out of the way of an oncoming truck.

For a while the road is free from traffic. So they start to walk nearer the centre of the road. Nearing Lashina's farm they see bags of palm kernels white against tree trunks stretching over five metres on either of the roadway. Next to the bags of oil palm kernels, are baskets and baskets of pineapples.

"I hope these aren't my pineapples Lashina is getting ready to sell!" Ekuma shouts.

"Hum Hum! I told you so!" Falala replies.

They arrive at Lashina's farm. At an intersection near the entrance, two narrow paths diverge. Not sure which way to follow, the women take the path to the left hoping it does not lead to the farmhouse. They reach the centre of the farm. They start harvesting fruit and filling their baskets. They are almost at the point of harvesting all the fruit at the centre of the farm when Lashina's wife, Ayie, catches sight of them from a vegetable patch she was tendering with the help of her young son, Musa.

She comes out behind them and shouts, "What are you women doing here?"

Her son concerned, stands by her.

Taken by surprise, they spin around sharply and face her.

"I am here to collect the balance of the pineapples for which I have already paid Lashina, your husband." Ekuma answers for the two of them.

"Lashina does not allow anyone to enter his farm without his permission and no harvesting can be done without him being present," Ayie says brashly.

"That is his business." Ekuma retorts. "My business is to harvest what is due me today! Your husband turned my brother back yesterday, saying that there were no ripe pineapples to harvest. Look at the line of baskets filled with ripe pineapples on the roadway near the farm. I have been told that he has been selling to buyers from the juice factory regularly, but he keeps telling me that he has run out of ripe fruit. I know this is a ploy to reserve the rest of the harvest for your own business. That is not going to happen, Ayie!"

"No? You'll see."   Ayie stands in the middle of the pineapple plots and begins to clap her hands and throwing insults at them. Her eyes are red with fury. Her lips tremble as she forces out the vile words.

"You should be ashamed of yourself," Ekuma speaks. What kind of a woman are you!"

Ayie continues insulting them. She wipes off the streams of sweat rolling down her bare arms with her *lappa* and halts for a while.

"Well," Falala says in a low voice to Ekuma, "The time does arrive when every aggrieved person has to face his or her provoker. That time has come for you, Eku."

Ekuma turns round and moves towards Ayie. She looks her in the eyes and says, "Your husband is a cheat and a robber. You know that he has been harvesting most of what's left of the ripe fruits since I was last here to collect my supply, and you have the audacity to come after me and stop me from collecting the rest of what he owes me!" Ekuma exhales air through her teeth. "Sheeeeeor!"

Ayie moves closer to Ekuma. She gives Ekuma a nasty look.

"Let me see how you are going to stop me! Ayie."

Ayie grabs at her dress and pulls her back. Ekuma loses her balance and recovers as Falala reaches out and stops her from falling. Falala then pushes Ayie away. Ayie returns, shouting, "Thief! Thief!" She tries to hit Ekuma, but Falala stops the blow and hits her on the chin.

Musa, Ayie's son starts to cry, seeing his mother hurt in the fight with the two women. "Mama, leave them! Mama, leave them! I am going to call Papa," he yells and runs away from the farm.

The scuffle continues for a while. Then Ayie, realising that alone she will not prevail against the women, unleashes again, a barrage of harsh invectives, picks up a handful of stones to throw at the women. Before they can react to her attack, she turns and runs in frustration towards the farm house. "Lashina will soon be here and will get the police after you!" she shouts.

Running back to the farm house Ayie trips on a tree stump and falls. She feels the pain in her left leg and knows there is a serious break somewhere above the knee. She cries, "Aye! Wai O Ya!" She attempts to stand and cannot. As she lies on the ground between rows of ripening pineapples, she sees a poisonous snake slithering among the fruit. It springs at her with head raised. Unable to move, she strikes at the snake's head with her head tie and misses. The head tie wraps round its neck. She panics and pulls at the head tie intending to throw it and its entrapped menace away from her. Her move draws the legless killer closer. In one swift leap from the bundle of cloth, it strikes and bites her in the neck. Ayie feels the sharp pain and slowly sinks into unconsciousness. In a matter of minutes she was dead.

Ekuma hears the cry and says to Falala, "Whom does she think she is fooling calling out like that?"

"She may be calling for Lashina," Falala says.

"Yes O! Let him come, we are ready," Ekuma replies.

Unaware of the accident they proceed to harvest until they have got all they are due. They take the narrow bush path that borders Lashina's farm and head for home. As they move further into the bush, they hear noises coming from the direction of the farm house.

"Listen Eku, they are singing hunting songs," Falala says.

"They are coming after us as if chasing *fretambos*[4] and squirrels," Ekuma tries to put a calm voice to words which express her disappointment at the steps Lashina is taking to prosecute his devious cheating game.

Suddenly, the singing and shouting from the crowd suddenly stopped. Then within seconds they hear a different pitch of voices rise from the crowd. They are cries of sorrow. People in the crowd are calling out Ayie's name over and over again.

On the farm, Lashina was leading a crowd in pursuit of the women trespassers, when he comes across Ayie's lifeless body stretched out among the bushy plants. Startled by this unexpected sight, the crowd stop their chanting, drop their sticks and machetes and start a chorus of wailing, calling out Ayie's name. Some of the women run to the village centre to raise an alarm. The headman, village elders and a crowd of curious villagers rush back to the farm to view the scene.

On seeing the body of his wife Lashina screems. Then he tells the crowd, "This is the work of Ekuma and Falala from Masanta. Musa is a witness. He told me that he saw the women viciously attacking Ayie when she stopped them from harvesting my pineapples."

These women are dangerous murders." The headman declares. "Let's go hunt them down immediately," the crowd shouts.

"Those women murdered my wife to conceal blatant theft," Lashina cried out in obvious grief. "Why! O Why! Why do they have to do this?" he says with tears in his eyes. Composing himself, he adds, "Headman, let us mobilize the strongest of our men in the village and move quickly to catch these murderers and robbers before they reach Masanta. This village owes me their support and I rely on you to help." "You can rely on me," the headman replies. "We shall leave now. My deputy will see that the corpse is taken to the village clinic for examination by the district doctor and obtain a death certificate, while we proceed to chase the villains. This is the doctor's clinic day in the village."

"Ekuma and Falala are dangerous murderers." The headman declares.

"This death must be avenged immediately," the crowd yells out.

" As they walk on Ayie says, "What do you think is happening back there with the crowd calling Ayie's name?" Falala asks.

Ekuma says, "We can't worry about that right now. Whatever it is, it puts more space and time between them and us."

"That crying means something has happened so serious that they have to call off the chase"

"Maybe. We'll find out later."

Ekuma and Falala proceed to walk further away from the farm.

They reach an opening in the bush and pass through a

track firewood cutters have cut in the bush to access the clearing from the main road to Masanta. They move quietly along the track to the road. They reach the stream on the outskirts of Masanta, where women and children are washing clothes. As soon as the children see them, they rush to help carry their harvest of pineapples to their house.

Arriving home exhausted, they sit on a bamboo couch on the veranda. Ekuma stretches out and rests her legs on a stool. Suddenly, loud cries and shouts from the road float in from the crowd.

"You cannot take the law into your hands and threaten to kill the women because you believe that they are responsible for Ayie's death?" The town chief was heard shouting as the crowd moves closer to the house.

"They too have taken the law into their own hands by illegally entering Lashina's farm, stealing his harvest and killing his wife," a man leading the crowd shouted.

The town chief moves to the front of the crowd and stops them. For a while they listen to him. "I have listened to you and understand your grief, but this is a matter for the police," he speaks with an authoritative voice.

"Not this one," the crowd roars contempt. With sticks and machetes in hand, they storm past the chief and stand in front of Ekuma's house.

"You thieves and murderers come out or we will burn your house down with all of you inside."

Falala stands and sees the Masanta town chief trying to restrain a crowd. She sees Lashina among them, advancing towards their house.

Ekuma whispers, "Come let's move away from here!"

Falala whispers back, "Ayie is dead!! They say we killed her."

The crowd begins to surround the house. The women move from the veranda into the house and pile every piece of furniture they have against the door and sit on the floor against them. They let the children who were still in the house leave through the back door. With sticks and axes they strike at the windows shouting, "Get out you two or be prepared to die in there!"

Two sturdy young men move forward and bang at the door trying to break it down. The crowd at the back of the house push in the back door. Ekuma and Falala rush into a nearby room and lock themselves in. They hear the crowd breaking into the adjacent room, then into the room opposite. They seem to be drawing nearer to where they are. They creep under the bed and lie still, waiting for the end. Then a thud on the door brought it down by the side of the bed. It sealed the entrance to their hiding place; but only for a brief period. As the attackers search the room, they hear the siren of the police vehicle as it drives into the village and arrives at the house.

The crowd start to throw stones at the house

"Keep clear off the house!" One of the police officers commands the crowd. "Please clear the way. This is now a matter for the police."

Defying the police, the crowd inside the house reach for Ekuma and Falala and drag them from under the bed. Just then, the police officers reach them and rescue the women from the violent crowd.

The officers lead the women to the village barray amidst

jeers and curses from the crowd. The most senior of the officers informs the Maposo town chief that the women will be held in custody for their own safety until charged. "The police will authorize a post mortem examination on Ayie's corps. The results of that examination will form the basis of any criminal charge," he explains.

Just as the police were leaving with the two women, the village nurse at Maposo arrives with the Deputy Headman of Maposo. The crowd notices them and allows them to pass through to the police guarding the women. Many in the crowd shout defiant remarks. "Tell the police we want their heads to take back to Maposo. Nothing else will satisfy us." Some of them try to breech the guard and reach the women, but two police officers hold them back.

The deputy headman from Masanta asks to speak to the senior officer in charge. He invites his headman, the Masanta town chief, Lashina and the Maposo village nurse to join him. He takes them aside and says, "I have the Regional doctor's report on the cause of Ayie's death. It states that Ayie died as a result of a snake bite. It further states that she sustained a fracture of the femur probably from a fall, after being bitten by the snake or when trying to avoid the attack." "This is a relief," the police officer sighs.

"The reaction of the people of Maposo to the incident is unfortunate," the Masanta town chief complains to the Masanta head man.

"Well, it would have been more than unfortunate if my men had not arrived in time to prevent a lynching," the senior police officer replies. Then he instructs the Maposo headman. "Now inform your people about the error of their judgement and get them to disperse. As night fell, Masanta was quiet again. In the quietness of the evening, Ekuma and her sister-in-law ponder over their day's trials. They receive friends and neighbours from the village, all offering sympathy and help with fixing the damage to their home.

The following morning Ekuma and Falala stay at home to count the pineapples they had harvested from Lashina's farm.

Sunday is always a busy day for sales at the 'Line.' Let's go to the stall!", Ekuma says to her sister-in-law.

"Yes! Let's go."

They set up their stall and there, like an apparition, Ekuma sees Mordu Koka approaching. She cannot believe her eyes. "Is that you, Mordu," she cries out in excitement.

"Yes, I want another basket of your sweet pineapples.

"It is going to be difficult" Ekuma declares

"Um! Why is that?" Mordu asks

"It is special stock! We almost died for it," Ekuma replies smiling.

"Is that so? Well we'll see! Bring it out and let me taste this stock, and see if it's as delicious as the last." Then jokingly he says "You'll tell me how you almost died for it later."

"It is no joking matter" she laughs. "Selling pineapples can kill in more ways than you can imagine", she gestures with her hands.

Falala watches the sudden excitement in her sister-in-law's gestures, the dimple in her cheek looks prominent as she reaches to fill a basket with lush pineapples, the line of customers forgotten. Mordu takes out some money from his pocket and hands it to her, saying "Ekuma, I'd like to set you up with another stall, a second business trading in bottled spring water. With water and pineapples, the risk of being killed will surely be low."

As Mordu drives off into the fading Sunday sun, Falala chuckles, "Love does happen even on the pineapple line."

Prince Kenny

THE GRAND REUNION

When Hudson finally broke the news to their mother that all six children and their spouses would be coming to Freetown for Christmas that year, Margaret was lost for words. Little did she know that apart from the fact that the children would want to enjoy Christmas in a much warmer climate, they were also going to give her a surprise seventieth birthday gift.

When she finally ended the call, Margaret sat down for a moment and pondered over what she had just been told. Indeed, she concluded, that she was a successful mother. She then remembered when her husband died some twenty one years ago and was left alone to take care of four girls and two boys: Hudson who was the eldest of six children had just passed the Advanced Level examinations with flying colours and was to enter university that year. Belinda being the second had also got her ordinary level results from St. Joseph's Secondary School and was to pursue sixth form at St. Edwards. Helen had been promoted to form four at St. Joseph's while Sylvia and Caroline were in forms two and one at the Annie Walsh. The youngest of the siblings, Peter, was in class six and was to take the Selective Entrance Exams the following year for admission to the great Prince of Wales which was the school their father attended. It was not a very easy task for her because she only did sewing. It was her meagre earnings that she used to give her children a very sound education.

When she finally regained her consciousness, Margaret raised her hands towards heaven to thank the great God of the universe for having made her a successful woman. As if that was not enough, she burst out into singing the hymn *"God moves in a mysterious way."* Having achieved all of that, she called her maid Mariatu and explained her joy to her. Like her boss, Mariatu was happy and she told Margaret that she was a great woman.

The following morning, the preparation started. Margaret had asked Mariatu to come with two other helpers so that they would finish giving a new facelift to the rooms and the parlours for the great reunion. All hands were on deck and in three days, they had finished doing their task. In fact, the house was not an old one as the children had completed it three years earlier. This was the house their father had started building before he died. As funds were not enough then, Margaret had to abandon the construction until the last child had got a university degree. When all of them had achieved their goals, they decided to finish the construction work and had their mother relocated to a much bigger house. Yes, it was really a big house with seven bedrooms, two living rooms (one with African furniture and the other with Western ones), a very big kitchen and dining and three garages. Moreover, four of the seven rooms had balconies attached and that gave the house a very conspicuous look.

In Europe and the United States of America, the atmosphere was also tense. With three weeks away to going to Africa, each child was trying to outwit the other. The unending telephone calls between them helped them to synchronize their preparations. They had earlier on shipped everything they would need for their stay; from the seven tier birthday cake to drinks and souvenir items they would give to guests and relatives at the party.

Another achievement in this planning was that they were all going to arrive the same day on board the same flight. They finally concluded to fly to Africa by Air France which was a direct flight. Therefore, Hudson and his wife Taibou and also Sylvia and her husband Gabriel had to fly from England to France. Caroline too had to fly to France from Holland with her Dutch husband Hans. Belinda who had got married to a Human Right lawyer Jacques and Peter who got married to a Spanish woman Prestinao had to equally fly to France from Ohio and Dallas Texas to meet the others. Helen, who was living in Paris with her husband Jimmy, had to take a train to Charles De Gaulles Airport in Roissy where they would meet their siblings and their spouses. It was great to have the flights from England, United States of America and Holland to arrive around the same time that day. There was ten minutes interval between them and within the next forty minutes, all six children had been reunited in the transit hall. When Hudson saw his sister Helen, he rushed and hugged her. He remembered six months earlier when he walked her to the altar of Notre Dame de Paris Cathedral and later handed over his sister to Jimmy. He did that because their mother could not make it to that wedding. In fact they had thought that Helen would never get married as she kept both education and career together. Here she was, having acquired three Master's degrees and was preparing her doctoral thesis in Human Resources. Her husband who was not as educated as she was did not mind her engaging in education as he was a B.Sc holder in Information Technology. After graduation, he did some specialization and got a job with the World Bank

Office in Paris as an IT specialist. For Hudson and the other siblings, Helen was their icon in the family as she was the most learned of them all. Yes, Peter too had a Master's degree and so did Hudson and Sylvia. Belinda did not bother to get a Master's degree as her husband was a great tycoon. He even told her to give up her work as accountant and stay home while he took care of her but she refused on the basis that the woman's place is not the kitchen. Caroline was a very successful business woman in Holland and she had business outlets in Dubai, Senegal and New York.

"My sister, since June, you have become ten times younger. What has Jimmy been giving you since then?" Hudson remarked.

"Brother, you always taunt me. I am still the same Helen you have known since childhood" Helen promptly replied.

Most of the passengers noticed that there was a kind of reunion at the airport as the hugs and kisses and laughter left some impression on the minds of others travelling that morning to Sierra Leone.

When the aircraft eventually touched down at the Freetown International Airport, there was a great sigh of relief especially for Peter and Belinda and their spouses who had travelled the farthest. They had flown eight hours to Paris and now they had added another six to their flying time. Their mother was at the airport together with their cousins Jamestina, Eugenia, Naomi, Ainajogor, Emmanuel and Joseph. Each of those cousins drove to the airport in order to facilitate the transportation process. Having gone through the formalities at the immigration desk, it was Caroline who was the first to come out. She rushed and hugged her mother. While she did that, her hand bag fell on the ground.

Fortunately for her, Belinda was at her heels and she instantly picked the bag and gave it to her sister. The others did the same and it was a scene of tears of joy as their mother had not seen them all in one meeting since they left for greener pastures. Their cousins also expressed similar sentiments and when that finished, they moved their luggage to the vehicles which had come to ease that burden. Standing in one corner was Mariatu the maid. When Helen noticed her, she walked gracefully to her and hugged her. She equally thanked her for having stayed longer with their mother Margaret than all the other maids.

When they eventually got home, the celebration was amplified. Very close neighbours and family members who had been told about the arrival of the group, were already there. Hugs, kisses, snapshots and other similar gestures were exchanged. Jimmy was introduced to family members since he joined the family quite recently as Helen's husband. He was tall and dark and spoke very softly that if one did not pay keen attention to what he said, you would not get the words clearly. Hudson's newest wife, Taibou, was also introduced to the rest of the family because he had earlier divorced Chrispina, whom most of the family members knew. When Taibou was introduced, Aunty Charlotte raised some eyebrow because she was of Fula descent. Hudson who quickly spotted her resentment, pointed out the fact that she had been baptized and confirmed and was a practicing Christian. Moreover, she was not like most Fula ladies who would stay home and allow the husband to work and take care of her.

When everyone had gone, the children engaged their mother in a private discussion. Sylvia and Caroline who were very witty, started a conversation about her friends as they wanted to know who was to be invited to their mum's birthday. While the conversation continued, Belinda was noting the names of mum's invitees. They also told her about their success stories. First was Belinda who had mortgaged a house with Jacques. Then was Caroline whose husband was promoted to a senior position in his office. Sylvia too had something to write home about as she registered that she had got a salary increase because of a successful project she prepared. Helen the book worm said that she was happy to report that she finally enrolled in her Ph.D programme and was satisfied with her husband and job. When it got to the boys' turn, Hudson did not say much. He only said that in the New Year, he would be posted to serve in the Hague for a period of three months and his wife Taibou would accompany him.

Peter spoke and said: "My mother, my sweet mother, I am also grateful to you because you are the most dedicated mother on earth."

The mother who was so curious to know why, went on to ask the question: "Why did you say so son?"

"Mother, you taught us to be honest, fair, frank, patient and hardworking. That has seen me through my career and family life."

"Peter, I am happy that you paid attention to those values and I believe that all of you will now say I was right."

They all nodded to corroborate their mother's statement. After the pause, she continued:

"Initially, you may have thought that I was a bad mother but here are you today yielding your dividend in the different spheres you find yourselves."

When the closed door family meeting ended, the children did not have any difficulty in finding their rooms. Margaret had already pasted each couple's name on the different rooms according to seniority. Of course the last three couples were in rooms that had no balcony but that did not raise any problem as they had known their mother to be very just and equitable.

The three days that followed their arrival were more hectic than the previous ones. The boys did the errands to the brewery to pay for the special Maltina drinks their mother liked since they could not get any in the West. They went to the shipping agency to collect the goods they had shipped earlier and also went to pay the final tranche for the hall where the occasion was to take place.

The girls were occupied with distributing the invitations to the friends their mother mentioned and to family members. In addition to that, they went to the caterer to finish payment for her catering services and handed over the condiments that they had brought. Caroline and Sylvia went to get some ready-made African dresses for their mother, sisters, brothers, husbands and in-laws. They bought two outfits for each person: one was to be put on for the annual Christmas day service and the other for the cutting of the cake. They were appreciated for their choice by their sisters and brothers but kept everything in camera from their mother.

On Christmas Eve, Margaret had some premonitions about what was going on. When she inquired about the extravagant preparation, Hudson remarked that they were preparing to receive their friends the following day as it had taken a long time they had not spent Christmas as a family. That night, the new window curtains were hung and also the garlands and other Christmas decorations. The illumination was splendid and from a distance, one would think that a ship had come ashore to berth that night.

At midnight, the atmosphere changed. It was as if an eruption had taken place as the music was turned high and all the children came from their different rooms knocking at Margaret's door singing *"Happy Birthday to you, mama."* Margaret who had gone to bed an hour earlier, initially thought that something had gone wrong in the house. When she listened keenly, she concluded that the singing was for her. She finally opened the door and to her greatest surprise, the six couples were standing in order of seniority, each having with a special gift.

Margaret was dumbfounded and could only express that with tears of joy. As each couple presented their gift, they made wishes to a wonderful mother. Peter could not help but cry and cry as he was referred to as *"mummy's boy."* His hug was the longest of all the children and when they finished that part of the ceremony, the celebrations started. They had done it in such a way that their cousins were asked to come to their house after midnight. Margaret was only lost in amazement at what was going on. She still thought that she was dreaming.

In the morning, there was so much rush as they did not want to be late for the annual Christmas day service at St. George's Cathedral. By 8:30 am, all was set and their cousins, who had slept at their house at Leicester Village, drove them to church. Within twenty minutes, they had arrived at St. George's Cathedral. Hudson and Peter saw their chorister friends and went to introduce their spouses to them. Helen too saw some of her childhood friends. Among them was

Clare who had put on a lot of weight. When she saw Helen, she was so happy and in two minutes, they exchanged contacts. Belinda, Sylvia and Caroline also remembered some of their Sunday school friends and spoke to them equally.

The service was well attended and among the famous hymns sung were "Christians Awake" and "Joy fills our Inmost Heart today." Climaxing that service was a special prayer which was offered for those born on Christmas day. Margaret was among those who majestically moved to the altar for prayers.

On her way to her seat, Melrose, one of her Mother's Union friends, said: "I wish you double congratulations: one for your birthday and the other for your sons and daughters who are here with you."

"Sister, I myself, I'm perplexed as they only told me that they were coming three days before they arrived. It was a real surprise to me. We shall talk more at the end of the service."

They did not spend much time after the service as they had to rush home and prepare for the major event that day. They ate what their mother had prepared but did not tell her that they were going to celebrate her birthday in grand style. By four thirty, they told their mother that they would like her to have lunch with them at Hotel Jenrince, which was situated near the famous Lumley beach. Like any proud mother, she wore the dress she put on to church that morning. Their cousins' cars were still at their disposal and when everyone was dressed, they drove to the hotel. No one said anything about a big birthday spread for mama. They finally got to the hotel and as mama drew near, she saw her friends and close family members seated. The hall was resplendent as the lilac and white table decorations and seat covers gave a touch of class to the event. Seeing all of this, Margret turned and asked her closest friend Mariana this question:

"What are you people doing here, sister?"

"Margaret, don't behave as if you don't know why. You invited us here and you are now asking what we are finding here?"

It was then she realized that her children must have played a trick on her. As she continued moving to the far end of the hall, she saw *"Happy seventieth birthday posters"* on the walls and balloons with the same inscription. She then called her son Hudson and expressed her feelings:

"Son you nearly killed me with such a shock. Why did you do such a thing without informing me. At least I would have put on a better dress and also helped with the catering?"

"Mama, today is your day and we did not want you to bother yourself. You are our queen today so sit tight and enjoy yourself. You mentioned about dress. It will surprise you that we have everything you need here. Helen has all the attire we have to put on in the car she came by."

O thank you my son. You don't know how much I appreciate you all. I will definitely tell people when I have the opportunity to do so."

"Then you have to respond to a toast that will be proposed to you. So you can tell them that. For now, just relax and enjoy your day."

They all got changed like Hudson had said and in thirty minutes, the programme started. There was a lot of food and drinks for the hundred and fifty invitees. In fact the food was served in a buffet lunch and everyone had to choose what he or she wanted.

Climaxing the event was the cutting of the cake and the

toasts and speeches. Most people had thought that Margaret would just cut the cake with her children and leave out the sons and daughters– in-law. To their greatest surprise, it was the reverse. When she was called to cut the cake, the sons and daughters–in –law walked to her and did the cutting with her. There was however a second cutting. That was a very unique one. All the children with their spouses stood behind one tier of cake each and had knives. Behind the seventh tier was Margaret alone. When Dennis, the chairman gave the cue for them to cut the cake, it was so marvelous to see all seven knives go down at the same time. It was as if they had rehearsed that type of cake cutting, although it was a spontaneous act.

Responding to the toast proposed to her by her cousin, Babatunde, Margaret acknowledged the guests who had been invited. She also expressed her sincerest gratitude and appreciation to her children who organised the wonderful show. She intimated that they are the best children in the world and have made her proud in life by their successes in the different walks of life they find themselves.

The rest of the party was as merry as the first part. By 10 pm, ninety percent of the invitees had left. The rest were a mixture of the children's friends and very close family members. They stayed there until midnight when they eventually left. Driving back home, Margaret was still baffled at her children's gesture. She appreciated what they had done and wished that all children would emulate her children's kindness.

The remaining three days following mama's birthday were also full of activities. In the midst of the activities, the children did not forget to get a great deal of African food stuff which they would need upon returning to their respective countries.

New Year's watch night was also splendid as they went to the traditional service at the Cathedral and when the service ended, they came back home with friends and cousins to have some festivity. That was their penultimate night as they were to fly out on the 2nd of January.

The departure was very emotional. It was really difficult for Margaret to accept the fact that the children had to return. The time they had spent with her went so fast that she did not wish them to leave so soon. In spite of that, they had to leave.

The sun was shining bright that day and the children surrounded their mother as she gave her piece of advice before they left. She remembered that same position some twenty one years ago when her husband died. On the day of the funeral, the children surrounded her to console her when the casket of her husband was about to be locked for good. Yes, they were very young then, but knew what it meant for a woman to lose her husband; and they did all to console her. It was not a funeral but a departure, which had a sombre atmosphere, as Mama was full with a heavy heart.

She concluded the prayer with much difficulty as it was full of sobs and moaning. Following that, was a word of advice to Hudson: "Hudson, you are the eldest, continue to look after your sisters and brother. You are now the father and mother."

"I will Mama, and we hope to come and celebrate your seventy-fifth birthday. We promise to always bring you laurels and will maintain those values you inculcated in us."

"May God help you to keep to your promise."

"And may God continue to keep you in health and strength Mama."

With these words, they left the house for the car. Helen who was very kind-hearted, slipped a fifty Euro note into Mariatu's right hand. The latter thanked her and promised to keep in touch with Aunty Helen. As it was a late flight, the children advised their mother not to accompany them to the airport and when their entire luggage was put in the cars, they left the house for the ferry terminal in order not to miss the ferry to the airport.

Gbanabom Hallowell (ed.)

Delphi King

ALONG THE MARINA

The sea is exciting
The breeze invigorating
The senses it stirs
To their profoundest sensuous depth
My flesh exposed it caresses
The invigorating gentle breezes
That blow in from the exciting sea
And I tingle at the touch.
My heart it races
My mind embraces distant places
I dream interesting situations
Where meet the sea, the breezes, you and I.

THE MYSTERY OF MAN

The depths of being
The unsoundable depths of being
The profundity of being!
Who can tell emotions strong
Lurking concealed behind the fleshly screen?
Who can say the sufferings borne
In mute subservience
Subservience mute
To father destiny
Hard relentless pushing?
The depths of being
More secret than the ocean bed
More lofty than illusive skies on high
The mystery of man!

THE VOICE OF AFRICA

The voice of Africa—
The roaring thundering
Voice of Africa
Will be heard!
The voice of Africa—
The mighty forceful
Voice of Africa
Calls to the world;
Across the forest rainy
The rich savannah grassy
Across the vast Sahara comes
The mighty voice of Africa
To the world!
A world engrossed in thoughts of war
A world where reigns suspicion fear
A world of tottering peace.
The voice of Africa
Will cry out
Pleading for peace and sanity
To rescue errant Humanity.

The voice of Africa
The roaring thundering
Voice of Africa
Must be heard!

Agyeman Taqi

CORRUPTION

Corruption...eating the discarded remnants of our moral fabrics...
Or have our morals been misplaced?
It seems that this is the case...
As the corrupt and corrupted are constantly rewarded.
Maybe we have been misled into fighting a losing battle...
When will it end?
When thievery is totally accepted as normal?
But how can this be?
Our Books teach us otherwise...
Then what is it?
Are we doomed?
What is this mess?

OH SWEET SALONE

Oh Sweet Salone, where art thou hidden?
I have searched tirelessly, in vain, for thee…
Only fleeting memories come to me,
Of serene nights devoid of growling 'Tigers',
Taps gushing with crystal clear waters,
Smooth paved roads with proper sewers,
Not pothole-ridden from neglect and old age,
And no rancid stench from stagnant garbage.

Alas! My search may be at a grand finale,
For I hear rumours, of sightings of thee…
Glimpses of brightly lit streets that are refuse free,
Of a new dawn, as the crimson sun rises,
Above the fronds of the wilting palm trees.
Respect for thy neighbour and the rule of law,
These are some of the things they say 'we saw',
Oh Sweet Salone show me where thou at hidden.

Leoneanthology

Elizabeth L. A. Kamara

THE HARMATTAN

The cool dry wind
Unsought, unwelcome
Or welcome,
Here, all the same.

The air is dusty
Faces, shoes, clothes
Doors, windows, furniture
Dust everywhere.

The face is dry, the skin is dry,
Lips appear lifeless.
Rough, chopped.

Voices become hoarse.
The throat is sore.
The nose is blocked.
Mucus filled.

Rapid drying of clothes,
Nursing mothers are happy.
Diapers are all dry,
Baby clothes and towels.

The cool dry wind
Slaps on the face,
Hits on the back,

Leoneanthology

Claws bones.
Leaves everywhere.
Fallen, abandoned.
Dust everywhere,
As wind gathers momentum.

Doors refuse to close.
Swollen with pride.
Impregnated by the cool dry wind
Of the Harmattan.

Gbanabom Hallowell (ed.)

THUNDERSTORM IN FREETOWN

Trees fall,
Roofs fly
Fences fall
A boat capsized.

A mad rush of the wind
Voracious in its fury
At Portee
A great cotton tree
Accepted defeat
It rushes to the earth.
Rushing some human
Beings to make peace
With the earth.
Other trees dropped down.
Trees and men,
Subservient
Unwillingly
Embrace the cold
Earth,
Which gladly welcomed all.

The angry wind conspired
With the turbulent sea
Lifted the boat, like

A piece of paper
Overturning it.
In that cold, salty water,

The victims lives are
Stolen.
Snuffed out.
Cut.
Off.
From this earth.
The sea, their graves.
Food for worms.
Food for fish.

In another part of town.
A fence collapsed.
Collapsed and killed
More of God's creatures
No prayers,
No farewell
No will.

At Moriba,
No compromise, no delay,
Roofs fly,
All over the place

As if a magician
Was conjuring the roofs
To up and away.

At the back of my house
The trees violently sway
This way and that.
Dancing in a frenzy
Dancing to some unheard
Music.
The trees bend
Listening, perhaps, for the call
The call to earth
But no call came
Save the sound of the wind,
With no particular message
The ground littered with leaves
Cut up
Bits and pieces
Like cassava leaves
Which refuse to succumb
To mortar and pestle

In the living room
My family
Frightened

Leoneanthology

Watching the dust stand tall
And praying for the rainbow.

FOURTEEN ATHLETES MISSING

Fourteen athletes missing
After commonwealth games.
Who cares about their names?
They believe it a blessing.

Demand a share of the wealth
Which they believe not common
In a country where athletes run
Give the slip in health and stealth.

In a land of hunger and thirst
Sierra Leoneans trust in God
Boarding the bird, giving the nod
Bearding the lion as they must.

They run, not taken aback
Fleeing malnutrition, rot, starvation
Disease, frustration, filth, deprivation,
In this land of tacks and lack.
They hide in a land of milk and honey
The world not green in Sierra Land
They have the hand and wand
To transform all into bread and money.

In for a rude awakening?
In for a glorious birth?
God grant them such mirth
Protect them from thunder and lightning.

: **Oumar Farouk Sesay**

I LISTEN

I listen to the sound of silence cascading on the ridges of their souls
like dew on a pond of lilies
I listen to the twang as the veins of their nape snap
from the weight of the world crouching on their shoulders
I listen to their spirit scampering to sit on the world
I listen to the implosion within their soul
I listen to the thrumming of their first steps
I listen to the stampede of feet as they run life's race
I listen to the faltering steps as they retreat from the race
I listen to the butterflies flapping wings in the rose gardens of their souls
I listen to the wind whistling solo song like a blend of flute
I listen to their dreams spluttering on arid land of reality
I listen to love roaming acres of need dreaming of love
I listen to the beats between their heart beats
I listen to the crescendo of their cries muffled in sighs
I listen to the platter of tears dripping in the amazons of their souls
I listen to the cadence of the sounds of our land
I listen to the cacophony of their agony screaming in their eyes
I listen to screeching of the mind of poets like nib on paper
recording the symphony of silence

I listen to myself listening to all the sounds
melting to a symphony of eulogies
I listen to my wish for a Ballard to drown the eulogies
I listen to the sounds of smiles ripping the frown on their
faces with the jaws of the drums of the harvest season

I listen to their sighs surfing the rice fields
I listen to their thoughts gliding the glades of their soul
I listen like a poet to capture the essence of their existence
I listen and I listen

THE OLD MAN ON THE ROAD TO REGENT

Every day the old man walks the road to Regent
with holes infest jean and jersey glued to his body
like the worn out bitumen on the pothole ridden road.
Perhaps it was the road that walks on him
For the sole of the road left foot print on the footpath of his
    soul
The stampeding sole of the road on his soul path
drown the pattering of his frail footstep
The thrumming of the road; a tremor on his memory
His mind spews the content of his soul on the road
The nauseous road spews its content on his soul
drenching his memory in a sewer of memories
like the torrent of footsteps eroding the road
The sole of the road tramples his soul
His soul and the sole of the road became soul partners
bearing the brunt of stampeding feet of bygone generation
Like Wordwoth's old man in Resolution and Independence
The old man on the road to Regent plucks consciences for
    leeches
In the moors of the souls of travelers on the road to regent
Leaving travelers of the road to Regent pondering
on how the old man became like the road to regent
    Trodden,
Down trodden

A CRY FOR MADDIE

for Madeleine McCann

I hold a cry in my soul
It is ebbing through the tears
Surging forth from tunnels of turmoil

Shoring in the inner shores of my being
Where the hollering of stolen children
Stole my soul like their stolen soul

I hold a cry for Maddie rumbling like a quake
To spew the torment of stolen children
Buried in cemetery of inhumanity
Where the vicar of our silence keep vigil

I hold a cry for the pain ravaging her mother
as she Lives in shadows embracing shadows,
Chasing silhouettes
And singing lullabies with a plunk of a dirge
For her living yet dying child
And dying yet living Maddie

I hold a cry for the unspoken word
between her parents as they talk without talking
And their ears deafen by screaming silence
Insomnia like an Alcatraz warden guide their sleep
And they die in their living and live in their dying

Leoneanthology

I hold a cry for Maddie as she wakes up at night,
In the vast tomb of inhumanity

Shifting debris to glimpse at the twinkling star
And sending a barren cry to a Mum
clutching a festering hope
Like the sores in the conscience of humanity

I hold a cry for the moment of her waking up
In the tomb of inhumanity
to live the death of a stolen child
I hold a cry for the lie they told her
And a cry for the hurt the lie left in her

I hold a cry for the parents
As they reconstruct the world on wishes;
Piling guilt in their soul for living life
As Maddie pine in the hands of evil

I hold a cry for the unanswered cry
Of Maddie crying out to us
As we tug our Maddies in bed with kisses
While she contends with a serpent hiss
As her kiss waste in an empty room

The tears of my cry rots

Suffocating the nostrils of my soul
Choking life from my being
Yet at the edge of my cry I still hold a cry for Maddie;

A cry for stolen children
A cry for their parents
And a cry for the lords of the outpost of humanity
Feeding the cries of my cry

TEARS

Torrent of tears pouring from the ocean of my soul
Lashing the banks of my eyes and rescinding
To the gorge within me
Gathering debris of emotions littering my souls sphere
For the many suffering in the outpost of humanity
Confluence of tears for refugees and orphans of refugees
And refugees of orphans
A watershed
I am drowned in the vortex of their anguish
I shed their tears alone in my loneliness
Their tears carved a Nile on my face
My mouth the sea for the river of tears
I chew their tears the salt of their pain embittered me
The anguish of their torment a desert in my soul
The wrinkles on the face of their tired dreams mummifies
me
The insipidness of their dead hopes nauseates me
I swallow their tears and their tears drown me
I become a thunder storm of teardrops
Dripping with torrents of metaphors
The River Rokel of my soul is flooding
I am drowning to write the tale of their tear drops
flooding the land
The tears of the lady of the night at Paddy's night club

selling pleasure on bowls of sorrow in the marrow of her soul
The tears of Soriebah the fisher man

Returning home to an ailing wife
leaving behind fishing net stuck to a Korean trawler
The tears of Barome gang raped and tongue raped for being
    raped
The tears of Jane yielding to the professor to make the mark

All their tears tear apart my teardrops to torrent of
metaphors for posterity to hear their cries
To smell their tears
To fell the fire of their undreamt dreams
To taste the bitterness of their anguish
This surge of tears drowning me
Is the tears of the pain of humanity seeking vent
In the eye lid of my verse

Isa Blyden

Gbanabom Hallowell (ed.)

THE WAILING WINDS

Marong whistling echo
hollow, high above cascading
murmurings of Charlotte falling
on black iron: rising stones in the
mist of a disappearing
             confluence...

Leoneanthology

RO-MARONG

Somewhere nestling in her coastal
depths is paradise, where many know
that secret path along which her
God whispering would walk as
beast, fowl, and a neutered Adam listened.

At a word, male and female had been
sent off to multiply, increase, replenish
the earth of what it might have lost in
winds blowing unintelligible utterances
over desert and plain vacuous, arid.

Beneath those once primordial pure
whisperings, moss now gross grows
groveling green so, Abraam, prostate
unleavened, hearing impaired, heard
in their stead steady coveting
clawing like lice in unshorn sheep.

And such tales! Mendacious, flawed
misleading millennia telling misdirecting
psyches unsuspecting, while listening
ears of an unsleeping Sphinx: her
watch on dunes undulating across
desolate places; her fingers calibrating

ruby pulsing through arteries beneath
ebony; her breath rising

to fall stilling Caucasian cacophony of charred
rust ridden faggots, sanguinary dust erasing
with one whisper primordial sins of
Pharaohs--tall preeminent African
heads unbowed, from deserts arid
rising…

KASSEH...THE BAI'S ACCOUNT...

In Port Lokko.

Round, small, white or red clay huts.
Dark interiors. The master bedroom like a granary.

In the depth of oil palm forests did the chiefdom flourish
far from the coast of Barbera and Bances where slaves
factoried yet, were shuffled away to await cargo
ships in cold caves spring water freezing
their naked soles, trickling from their heads,
mingling with the salt trickles from wondering
eyes watching as they loomed brooding from
the mist...

(Crimes against African humanity yet untrialed...)

And to this kingdom far removed from such
madness arrived *or-potho* in the rising mist
of *presork* to tarry with neither tongue
nor script; his eye steady on covet.

Compassion stirred for his mute deaf jinn
who'd crossed waters he himself hadn't.
Hospitality prevailed over reason.
Or-potho dined on the Bai's bounty

thin bigoted lines of yellow bone briefly
slithering spittle on his fawn and feign;

Presork! His whining jinn fawning 'neath
his wisdom uttered,

*"Have ye the tax for your huts? Hermaj'sty's
wanting.."*

He watched the insolence glimmer in
The jinn's eyes; his cheeks shining from
generous helpings of oil palm and yuca
those many months untaxed, woven

cotton coverings over his loins
and chest; tgoat
grease concubines nightly massaged
plump white soles with; his whining
filling the rustic silence…

"Have ye the tax? Her Majsty's wanting!"
"Ra presork ar dae?!"

The Bai remembering his children's
cries of *"Mamour O! Mamour O!"*
at Fuuta Fula flogging; driving them

Leoneanthology

to settle a coast of wailing winds
Irate, the Bai rose to dispatch scouts
griots to sound drum and cow horn,
bondo to sharpen shield and nail,
Then donned his regal
                ronko...

P.M. Wilson

THE LOST LOVE

We were once lovers seeking earth's paradise.
Under a tree, by the lake's sparkle did we make love.
I reminisce the long but yet so short days gently caressing
your head in my arms
And shifting my fingers through your soft locks.
As I stare into your pearly eyes my love for you culminates
stronger than ever
Your body, so enriched like the walls of the Persian palace
and slender like the Nile
Your lips so smooth and tender like the wings of a dove in
flight.
And when words are spoken from the two
Your voice so ever *douce*, like the autumn leaves
On the rigid grass caressed by the whispers
Of the gentle breeze drifts me away into an unknown fantasy
Where harps of harmony flourish the air
Your hands so fond and moist, a modicum of food
From the tip of your fingers fed to a warrior could quench
his thirst
And satisfy his hunger. Your love could give him victory
over battles
You must have the image of the first woman ever created
For her existence was solely to fritter away man's loneliness
And you my love were created just for me
To fill my life with all there is to desire, and to cast my
Burdens away as I yield to your passion.
Love couldn't live inside a woman as love lives inside you

But affection was curtailed
W were kept apart by fate. You were
Snatched away from my sight
Taken by raiders from the distant world

Like an infant taken away from its mothers breast, so
Were you taken away from your lover's arms and into the
hands of strange men
Lifted on a horse you vanished from my sight
Into the wilderness where beasts and barbarians roam
But I fought with all the power that was bestowed upon me
from the heavens to win you back.
But I was overcome by their swords and whips
You vanished along with your love
I turn to the lake under the tree
Where we once played love, a vision strikes my sight,
An image of Nefertiti calling me to her arms
Yet I look clearly, it is just leaves and branches swaying.
You are not there my love
My eyes cry tears and visions of you are frequent
There is no mountain that can conceal you from me, and no
battle that I can't win to see you again
I will find you one day, and once more you shall be mine.

LONELY NIGHTS SPARE ME NO MORE

In this life transcends illusions, we are mere passing souls

LONELY NIGHTS SPARE ME NO MORE

Without your warmth and touch my days run cold

LONELY NIGHTS SPARE ME NO MORE

Like a callow in the haze without your love I am a coward that yearns for heaven's bliss

LONELY NIGHTS SPARE ME NO MORE

But if I may live forever, life would be senseless without your mild and tender kiss

LONELY NIGHTS SPARE ME NO MORE

Gbanabom Hallowell (ed.)

Josephine Ansumana

HOLIDAYS

I

Holidays are happy times
Spent with loved ones
Reliving happy memories
When the cares of the world
Are laid to rest
Until the illusion fades
Away and the reality returns.

II

But I have never been lucky with holidays
That is when the shutters fall
And the demons are free at last
To torture my mind, and tear my heart apart
I fear their accusations and the
Loneliness they bring, cause no one
Shares my days, but my tortured soul.

III

The worst experiences in my life have all
Happened around the holidays
The very first Christmas eve I recall
I guess I was about five
I torched the hair on my head
With a lighted candle.
But for our good neighbor "Connah."
I could have been scarred for life.

IV

The next was when I came home from school
Expecting holiday gifts as before
Sadly, there were no new dresses,
No toys, or presents from my parents.
That year, my father went private
And times were pretty rough then.
They could not afford the extras
They made no big deal of it.

V

Then came the time my dad was so ill,
I had to rush him to the hospital
I came home from University then
I matured overnight into a responsible woman.
They took him to the Emergency ward
Then to the Intensive care unit it was.
Admission and tests they ordered
Operations scheduled two days later.
I prayed as I never had before,
It all happened on Christmas Eve.

VI

Then there was the year I had
My daughter on Halloween's day
Post natal blues, I struggled with

Highs and lows where my mood swings
But no one really cared then.

By Christmas Eve that same year
Her father and I were estranged.
My emotional journey started then.

VII
Then there was the first Christmas
I spent away from home.
And away from my daughter too.
My heart bled all the while
And I shed a million tear drops
All because of the million miles apart
It was then I lost the meaning of Christmas.

VIII
The Christmases that followed
Were no better since.
Each a constant reminder
Of a serrated and bleeding heart
A broken heart all hopes has lost
A mix of tears and sobs to ease my pain
My mind refreshed by faith renewed to
Expunge the anguish from my lonely soul.

IX

I fear holidays and what they bring,
A cry of anguish for wishful thoughts
For true love in silence, I hope and pray

My heart slowly bleeds for a lost love
While my very being tortured by
The pains of loneliness, quietly waits
For a new day soon to dawn

X

Holidays are happy times,
Like no other time of the year.
Their magic is real and simple and true
A time of giving, a time for sharing
A time of faith, hope, love and charity
Impossible dreams, wonder and fairy tales
A time of forgiveness and mercies given
Of divine love, freely given and miracles blest

THE VENDOR'S FLIGHT

Theirs is an "unholy" alliance
A love affair in turbulent seas
Like two "C" intertwined
She is stereotyped as
Worthless and no good
The scum of academia
She considers him a small mind
With a peanut size intellect
And a giant ego
She is an honest laborer
Made to feel undignified
In her labor
Il-treated and spat upon,
She is used and abused
By the lover she serves.
She wears his indignities
Like a scarlet badge
But the "client" they say
is always right.
Though she too is human
Deserving of respect and appreciation
All she ever gets are the constant
Crack of the whip, followed
By the lash of the tongue.

THE IMMUTABLE POWER
OF FOREIGN AID

I

Managing the great humanitarian aid is the
Worst form of North and South Dialogue.
A strategic form of neo-colonialism pursued
In the guise of humanitarian Assistance
Flooding the continent with all sorts of Aid!!!
A deceptive quid pro quo arrangement
Food aid in exchange for national control
Cheap goods traded for natural resources
Treating their hosts like satellite nations
Poking their noses where they do not belong
All in the name of the great humanitarian Aid.

II

"Don't you worry," said the North Pole
To the South Pole. "I have you covered."
"Covered! With what and from what?"
Asked the South Pole with a measure of doubt.
"I have you covered from poverty, diseases and wars,
I have you covered from floods, hunger and drought.
I have you covered with Euros, American Dollars
And British Pound Sterling notes.
All new, crisp and smooth to the touch,
Henceforth, your problems are over.
I have "you" under control," the North Pole replied.

III

"Oh! Ho! I see! How very generous," observed the
South Pole in a passive voice pregnant with meaning
"Are you really sure you are helping me up
Or are you just keeping me down? if I may ask."
"Oh! Then, I guess you did not get the *memo* after all!"
"Memo! Did I miss something?" echoed the South Pole
"Of course not, dear! We just decided that henceforth
I am your appointed guardian and mouth-piece,
With exclusive rights and power of attorney
To raise money for the poor, in your name,
And spend it on palaces and homes in my name,
 As a token of my love for you, in your name,"
The North Pole bragged, beating its chest.

IV

"AH! See how much they love us," the South Pole opined.
"They *love us so much*, they speak in our name
Then send their "people" to our land in our name,
On humanitarian *assignments* they humbly pledged.
 To speak for us, act for us and work for us in our name.
"*Equal Distribution of Jobs*" their policy stated
Exclusion and exploitation the mandate spelt.
Local clerks, drivers and housemaids--*fair distribution*.
"The fools can never tell the difference" they chuckled."

V

Extended vacations fully paid, you bet.
To laze around desolate never-ending stretches of
Windswept white-sandy beaches in our name
Sun-bathing halter tops and skimpy bottoms in sunny shades,
Speedos, thongs, skinny dipping in the deep ocean's swell.
Pedicure feet patter across rolling dunes of sand
Bleached tresses sway in rushing winds. As eyes gently
gaze into shimmering lakes, lagoon, waterfalls,
Gushing rivers and tempestuous waves.
 All done in a day's work, in our name.

VI

Transparency, Accountability and Due diligence
Their instruments of choice. Strategic principles well
    defined,
Ethics and Social Responsibility they never apply.
"We can damn well do whatever we please," the North
    teased.
"What did you expect? Of course we call all the shots
We gave you ten percent of *our money*, you better not
    complain
You either do exactly as we say, or we blacklist you.
What happened to the ninety percent, pray do tell

We are not at liberty- a "Non-disclosure" policy applies
 After all, it is our money," The North Pole argues.
"Ah! Yes! Indeed it is your money--Your money taken
Out in our name," the South Pole replies.
"But just so you remember it was our idea, after all."
"As long as you do not forget that this is our land."

Moses Kainwo

A LETTER TO
CORPORAL FODAY SANKOH[13]

dear mr sun-core
hold
and let the handshake speak
i know your lenses are blind to kailondo's[14] staff
i know your wavelength is deaf to kailondo's voice
but hold

innocent blood queries my throat
please field marshall
please president of another world
please chief justice of injustice
hold

touch wood
that you would grant the insane your sanity
the cocoa your freedom
the unborn your hope

please mr sun-core
hold
and let the handshake speak

---

[13] Corporal Foday Sebana Sankoh was the name of the man who led the rebels of Sierra Leone in the eleven-year old war (1991 – 2002).
[14] Kailondo was a famous Mende warrior from the East of Sierra Leone.

THE CULTURE OF PEEPING

Eyes

I

Those with gyrating eyes have prophesied,
That the eyes are openings on the side;
But entrepreneurs of the visible,
Shall trade their luck with the un-seeable.

The young are short-sighted from seeing too much,
The old are long-sighted from seeing so much.
Children peep to see with elderly eyes
Dancing adults in their love store and cries.

See them now blinking at photos at play,
While adults must blink their fanlight replay:
The ticklish world will unlock a window,
The greedy world will shut the gazer's show.

Little surprise some shutters are so thick,
Though lucent curtains serve the purpose pick:
Many a gazer will tick to street bells,
And choose not to be their sisters' angels.

II

Oh yes you can choose to see or not see,
Because death standing in that deafening knell,

Attracts a witness that is not witness:
Behind the window blinds the conscience stress.

I turned it on my mind over again,
Me too, I am not my sister's bargain;
I am her Lucifer[15] to chant her there,
And since no one beholds I shall not care.

Lucifer is in you my country bore:
Together we mused and our sister tore,
From the Gallery down to the Crypt,
And from the Crypt down into the street.

If by this token new perception drops,
Then the nation wins the cowering crops:
Elect a hoodlum and you have an imp,
There you'll survive with a well-earned gimp.

Let each goggle gauge a reverse gazing,
On the battered soul deformed from blazing:
Indeed a sorry darkness sits within,
And only when it rises will it spin.

---

[15] Lucifer is another name for Satan, the fallen angel (See Isaiah 14:12).

Rivers

I

Five great rivers the death comrades did cross,
To square up with the age-old peeping loss:
They broke the bridges and co-steered their way,
The strange navigators driven by pay.

An evening salute from death on the streets,
Was not so welcome to the peeping feet;
In fact the streets died with a woeful woe,
As they bled and wasted before the foe.

Their names were written in the book of pyres,
To choose their deaths in the face of hellfire:
They received the eye-bursting-dripping beads,
Or the gift of shirts with chosen sleeves.

New rivers began to flow the main roads,
Nameless rivers made of countless red loads:
My sister peeped and her eyes became blood,
Her letter of love was there in the flood.

Leoneanthology

II

Operation-no-living-thing had no date,
Or else this poetaster could not vibrate;
But Death sharpened the machete and cursed,
The blood flowed and got curdled in the nursed.

No one ever cursed like that heavyweight,
No one ever cried like that featherweight;
The two looked at each other in the eye,
And the new peeping game was cast in dye.

But there was no rhythm in the new song:
By the Atlantic Ocean there we sat up,
Waiting for a boat to sail or fly,
Anywhere on God's good terrain to swarm.

The river flowed on flora and fauna,
Shoppers jumping on to Noah's basket:
Some green some white some blue unseemly queues,
Singing how we exhaust thee in the blues

One mosquito that sucked the blood,
And became fat and burst open with flood:
It was rotten and not good for washing,
So it was drained and bottled in a sink.

Creation

Was this the way the universe began,
Or is it where the universe will dance,
In green and white and blue of any shape,
With lions unseen on mountains in cape?

The metaphysics of the guessed order,
Throws naiveté at the vexed founder:
And that imaginative family tree,
Is god-planted to harbour fleas.

The Cotton Tree of Flee-town is like a god,
Around whom the fleas converge day and night;
And every sober march re-routes from there,
So she is amply fed and dressed right there.

Where the green god stands there is flesh on bones,
There is hope on toes that the green god knows,
From daybreak to nightfall they come and go,
Lifting new symbols from the place below.

Not one burgher knows who proscribed with fire,
And I want to ask who lighted the tyre.
Who made the bad heart, I can only guess.
But who declared the war we should not now stress.

Leoneanthology

How can we know where knowledge is remote?
You press a knob and something is afloat,
You lift a finger and some figure drowns;
The bluecoat is there with his fingers cupped.

They say the Cotton Tree saw them chop dogs,
She must have also seen them bogging bogs.
But who can make her tell the faded tale,
When the truth itself has been painted pale?

The sold train track some travel curses banned,
The power now rests in the palm of the band,
This also is now in the poda handout;
But real power remains in the rear mouth.

Right around your base and just yesterday,
America waved in the nude by day;
And again yesterday like the other judge,
UNAMSIL[16] was baptising in the lodge.

And they said disrobe to enter the pond.
He took off a shirt and then the bell-bottoms:
Four shirts and four trousers on one body,
A moving wardrobe in fear of war folly.

---

[16] UNAMSIL: United Nations Mission in Sierra Leone

Story-telling Tree, receive the prayers,
Offered in jest as a test of the years,
Your children will come from obloquy and cry,
Forgive their past and from your glory spy.

You gave them a tongue and gave them a song,
You gave them the drug and gave them the time,
The chequered love of a chequered nation,
But the wheat and the tares must have options.

Seasons

The dries are not summer so call them that,
Winter and autumn each have their own flag;
They will come next year and always be first,
But will not spring where the reason is wet.

The tears in you will come as will the rain,
Because the soul is alive with the times,
And the charred remnants of battle will float,
T'announce the evidence of battered throat.

And one drunken gun-totter said to me,
"This is your own ambush brave pedigree,

Leoneanthology

Empty your pockets on a deserving angel,
The revolution is here first to sell".

"Was this the accord you promised to pour,
Hunger and thirst rained upon all the poor?"
I could not ask more that desperado,
The stooge of death ordered the thing to do.

Someone will hate the success tale you tell,
Someone will not stop despising your wealth;
But please succeed and retreat from the rest,
To hold onto excess will be a test.

Can present time annul past time and stay?
You cannot bat the ball and keep it—nay!
The aged say the times are new to them,
The young reckon but say their time is tame.

We don't even know who last left the shores,
Since the going is similar to coming.
Can you actually blame the move on one,
When in your heart of hearts you hate the one?

To appear they had to disappear,
But time will come though time was always here;

And time once lost is time forever gone,
As a deed done is a deed forever done.

Roses stand in dustbins and make them sweet,
We need one on this ground for wiping our feet:
Life now smells of the swift and the ugly,
True revolution will make the foolish holy.

Leoneanthology

LEBANON ON THE MOVE

Tantrums from the valley beneath
Are echoed repeatedly from above
If only
If only they'd retreat
Like Kingdom forces
With banner before missile

    You know
    Real peace
    Slipped through their fingers
    Like water in a sieve

Abess Alie-Samir[17] Esquire
Former diamond magnet
I salute you
Did I hear well
That one missile sent you home
To the Bacar Valley
Only for another to send you home
To the *Kambui Hills*[18]

Little did I guess
The conversion of a hilly life
Into a richer valley life

---

[17] Abess Alie-Samir: A made-up Lebanese name
[18] *Kambui Hills* is a range of hills surrounding Kenema Town, the town where diamonds are bought and sold in Sierra Leone.

Was an empty vessel
In the hands of choice and duress

I must add a tear
To your river of tears
In the tearing of a valley
Now seated on the epicenter
Of an earthquake
Measured since 1947
I see your face among the displaced
The dispossessed

When will a ruby stand
In that valley
To salute your signature in style
When will the history book
Be ready for your eyes
When will the children
Recite the verses of Omar Kayam[19]
When will a President truly say
They gave you a plot to plot your peace
When will rhetoric grant you
Permission to look at your gems

---

[19] Omar Kayam: Famous Lebanese poet

Maybe soon maybe not
Maybe the tears will dry up
Soon yes very very soon

Let us keep that
They say after dark the dawn
Let us keep that
They say the shadows of moonlight
Will roam and find rest
Let us keep that
They say the shadows under the rubbles
May not occur twice
Let us keep that
Or may they

Gbanabom Hallowell (ed.)

Fatou Wurie

UNTITLED

In melody
He is allowed to enter
staring into her
his
face is capped with pleasure
She simply looks simple.

Puddles.
She jumps into the puddle
Deeper than expected
Just like her hole.

Thrusting
Wider,
She un-becomes
he dances, latching at control.

They both fall into tangled cosmic imbalances.

It is winter
The chills aren't very kind,
She steadily smokes her cigarettes,
Drags real slow
memories melt
rapid rapidly.

She continues to inhale
he exhales
in his sleep.

Bitch.
He whispers sweet nothings into her ear stream
Her name is uncomplicated
Sit down,
Be good.
He doesn't notice she has a dog.
His mouth is greedy for her breasts
She simply looks simple.

THE PRIVATE LIFE OF WAR
Inspired by Susan Griffin's book called the Private Life of War

Birth. I choose to not tell my *protected* friends that I was born in a small house in a small village nestled in the small corners of Africa. I cannot tell them that we did not have running water, or that my grandfather died in a small colorless room—he was a man who came from a life of rags to one of riches and back to rags. Privacy is important to my family. We do not talk about fragmented family members who still reside in a time where proliferated guns, machetes and knives were central to the landscape and culture of a place they know as home. We are private. My friends, they cannot understand that the black child without arms that they see in media mediated images are byproducts of a war that demanded other black children become killers. War, it conjures images of men with weapons, of death, of blood, of the decapitation of family structures.

I see black corpses, Bosnian corpses, Jewish corpses—corpses that have lived in the small house I was born. I smell tears; they are the only signifiers and tellers of endured pain, of survival.

When I hear phrases like the *private life of war* a sad smile forces my lips into movement. War is never private; it may be pocketed and isolated but collectively we all mourn and grieve. Private is an illusion maintained by the powerful. Fools, we even tell those who return from battle that they too must maintain that illusion, their grief can only spill within, and if they cry, we will collect their tears and hide them. Hide, hide,

hide—hidden even if our visibly invisible limbs are reminders that we were once at war.

The little colorless house I was born in is a battlefield on its own. It has birthed, screamed, lost, and endured rape, trauma, laughter, community, strength, and mental breakdowns. It has housed dreams and bears witness to the deaths of the owners of those dreams.

There is no negotiating war. It is alive in the body; it seeps into our collective consciousness even when we try to forget.

2 months after invasion

Her hands they move methodically. Chopping she sits and chops.
Onions and sweet gravy engulf the corners of the room as Nana sits and chops: carefully, properly, and dejectedly. So intensely I feel her slip from the room.

It is a hot day. It is natural that large balls of sweat

roll down her oak brown skin, freely dropping into the skin of chopped vegetables. The sweat will act as sweet seasonings, managing to replace nostalgia. I am mesmerized by her hands, which she often moisturizes with palm oil. Nana had brought me into this world with those hands. She had opened my mother's legs to

bring me into the *dunnia*. The dunnia she says was gifted and mystical; we had to accept its gifts. Everything is a gift, Nana often says, everything, every being. *Alhamdulliah*. Her hands are now chopping dangerously.

I can feel the sun glare at us angrily for some archived sin we weren't quite sure we committed. The warm breeze that passes from time to time hushes us not to worry. So we sit. I, watching my grandmother chop. Her eyes are transfixed on the defenseless items sprawled on the chopping board and I become lost in a world of my stewing fears. We do not speak for we embrace without touching in the large brown kitchen located in the corner of Nana's small house.

It was here he had died that warm afternoon. The air I remember was sickly sweet and void of origin. It smelt like everything and nothing. It was here. Blood splattered on the walls colouring the bland brown. In this very kitchen. It is here food is cooked—feasts orchestrated and delivered at the highest of quality. Nana would inject animal fat into unfattened bodies hoping to give the impression of proper nourishment. She did her best to dispel the 'dying African child' stereotypes.

It was here little children were Bathed and spanked, loved and spared. The kitchen had gratuitously produced life while at the mercy of death's imminent presence.

I knew Nana was chopping for control.
I allow her be.
I remain lost in a sea of memories as beads of tears roll down my skin. Freely, they too transform into seasoning for the meat and vegetable Nana is chopping. It is here he died. It is here I was born. `Nana says everything is a gift.

Richmond Smith

Gbanabom Hallowell (ed.)

THE DEFENDER, my brother

I was four years old
Halfway into our 'SMITTISH 'code
Religious citations.
Pouring Libation
AS we hailed 'MARY' (Mother of Grace)
And 'JESUS CHRIST, our personal savor.
In my little Ghetto space

Screaming polythene bags
Half-full with 'Ghetto Rags'
And locally –made toiletries
('Charcoal, chewing sticks and 'fatu –sweet')
Herbal Tea, Spices and 'Green Patches'
Stashed into a handy –made sleeve
'Bo Gari', brown sugar and Maggie –source
Mixed with groundnut –oil and strong spices

Ahead of the Bus stop
Plenty of miles
Tearful eyes
Running Nose
Feeling COLD
And the 'battle song 'unfolds….

"The defender, my brother
Left home during the summer
Just the cigarette packet's addiction

Many targets

No regrets 'for a favorite action
Be bold, play it slow
And, if you weren't told
Life is sacred and golden
Problems always have solutions to solve them
Be tuff in December
Accept some defeats
No retreat, no surrender
Make friends till you are strong
And learn to bake your own bread, he said."

Beautiful smile and kisses
With fingers linger away from each other
Anticipates my hopeful wishes for a 'Big Brother'
As he disappears into the dusty road
The bully prepares his advances…
The defender, my brother
Left home early
But, now I am forty years old.'

THE OLD SHOES

These old shoes without soles
Are vultures in the rain that daily left me
Clutched under armpits across skies
To the dustbin of my life decaying

Daily, I squeeze my soul in to
These old shoes without soles
And the *'suck —teeths* of my steps
The insult of my life
Gather fingers to poke laughter in to my hurt
Big as the 'Cotton —tree'
By the former American Embassy
At Walpole Street.

Daily I hit Walpole Street,
Where Lincoln's Pajeros, B M Ws and Mercedes
Paraded in pomp
But, on the white —paints of vultures excreta.

These old shoes without soles
Are quite familiar with my adventures
And now my feet benefits
Resilient to obstacles and defeats.

DEEP SILENCE

Moments into my deep silence
Graphed with known sentiments
Nick Names, witnesses and soaring guilt
My heart sunk so deep …..

Collecting facts from steel faces
A herd of 'BLACK SHEEP '
Dog fights
Drug thrills
Bloody defeats
Money spills
And the 'street office' sometimes kills
My heart sunk so deep…..

Moment into my deep silence
Quit, dark and free
Sowing 'JAH' seeds
Beyond the depth of my heart
On rocky fields
Swampy creeks
Mountain peaks
Throughout many miles of bleakness and fitness
My heart sunk so deep….

Moments into my deep silence
Asking just one salient question with caution
Where are my brother and sister's keeper?

It was bad weather I
More lives claimed
Others were maimed
As we mourned the dead
And sometime is said
We all go to bed in tears
Sleep walking
Cheap talking
Dogs barking
Flip –flopping
Till my content swells into other continents
My heart sunk so deep....

Moments into my deep silence
Feeling aggrieved, tainted and wasted
Fainted with tears dripping upside—down my face
Watching my shoe lace
Neatly tied above the thatched ceiling
Awaiting the execution
Whilst, suicide offers a bride price
My heart sank deeper...

ENGLISH LANGUAGE

English language
Seems to be like wages for the English
Boy, Girl, Women, and Men
Seek to flip-scroll through all 'em pages
Although, it's a passage unto my pilgrimage
I 'll still take my time to build an image
That wouldn't tamper with my courage

Speaking in my mother's accent
Wouldn't cost me, not more than a cent
Nevertheless, it is priceless
This might seem so useless
If, I did fancy the sign language

The Asians, the French and the Persians
With other European misfits
Spend money, time in ages
Improving short sentences in stages
While seekers receive gifts as achievements
A bachelor degree, master and a PhD
A perfect set-piece that eludes
Human misery in retirement

Buying ivory
Before the discovery
The savagery in slavery
And a fine –tongue would make' Me' happy…?

English, English
Designed for the academics

Posh-English
Is for the indigenes

Broken –English
Is for the natives

A British fetish
That spreads across the savanna
Just like marijuana in Africa

Being part of your audience
Chilling with friends, family and relatives
And with my little English Experience
Coerced me to speak English Language
Which, is almost defeating
So let's say, *'aw di bodi'*
My personal greeting in krio
And *'tehnki'* to JAH
For beautiful Salone and the Creoles

If you have any qualms
With what you have just read
Please, be mindful of what others have shed
For the sake of the English Language

Fatou Taqi

WOMAN

    Born a girl
Frowned upon for a while
Learn to fight
Strive to succeed
Married off indeed
Dreams, plans, implement
Cook, clean, toil
For your man and your home as dependents

THE CORD

So attached...
...invisible pull
...invisible pain
...locked in a mother's womb
...when if ever can it be cut?
...struggles, attachment, dependence
...joys or sorrows of motherhood
...can a mother's role be redundant?

Gbanabom Hallowell (ed.)

Komba David Sandi

BIG MEN DO CRY

Fewer people come these days
to scheme, to cringe to genuinely mix.
His padded boots still squat in the hall
Her headscarf's draped on the hanger above....

They sit arm in arm in the still clear photo
timeless beings in timeless times...
is this the true love so few gain?
that eludes so many time and again?

Remembering the warm smile, even when tired
exacted by excited patter of a bubbly child.....
despite hours of toil from morning till night
on many occasions, from morning to morn!

You never expect that involuntary gulp
that sinking feeling then welling inside...
it's hard to stop the tears that flow
brought on by fond memories:
Big men, do cry!

REFLECTIONS

Do you remember years ago
when someone asked the price of peace?
Did you ask how much it cost
dirt cheap or was it really steep?

Answers come easy when one is young
but gain in girth and depth with age.

Did you ever give a thought
how much a price is really worth
that not only lives but minds are lost.....
not only foes but friends as well?

Do you remember years ago
when someone asked "what's in a word?"
when fair was foul and foul still fair...
when girls were boys and boys still girls?

Do you remember yes, do you recall
the ice warm hearts, soaking dry nights
grating melodies, tearful joys?
Some things we remember
some we'd rather forget.......
yet they're all still part
of what reflection brings.

FOR SAKE OF INNOCENCE

On a bus that day
a hungry sojourner on his way
at a food stop asks :

"Is it fresh? Is it well cooked?"

Between the jostle of thrust trays
 a tiny face appears.........
courage finally plucked
he shouts above the elder throng
chest puffed with pride:
"*Yes* they *are* fresh"
 they *are* well cooked - *my mum* made them!!"

The traveller notes his tattered shorts, well-worn top
 still laden tray........
 he'd wanted two instead buys ten
small change for him a lottery for the boy.

He declines an offer to take one free
smilingly assuring that ten would do.........
and when the bus slowly pulls away the lad waves and waves
till out of sight.

As the bus roars forth the traveler thinks:
what made the sale, what the excess buy?
the poverty, elderly advantage, the child's desperate appeal?
Or was it the faith, the unquestioned trust
 in an absent parent that had touched his wandering soul?

CHILD SOLDIER

I feel no joy
nor relief
just blistering calmness
Lull before the storm?

No it's not what I thought would be:
the triumph……gladness and release.

A funny little growing fear

They tell me there's a hell out there
some great hot hole where the evil roast
are cooked in their own belly fat?

Cold sweat runs down my spine now
my head beats like a drum…………
my breath is choking dust now
I feel so much alone!

I stroke my gun, my books,
my gun: it's all *their* fault
I scream within………….

Her burbling guts
his rancid ones
make me feel sick –
I spew!

Recovered I count 9, 10, 11…12 over there
13 in the bush…………………………..

The next class's neat
they cringe five deep
I shut the door
to drown the roar.

Oh holy so and so I cry
Please help me in my time of trial…..
Oh holy so and so I grin
And blast them all away!

REBEL ATTACK

I wish I was lying by the sea –
cool breeze green groves
sparkling white sand

I'd like to drink an ice cold beer
watch my team and listen young Ami sing.

I wish I'd finished my degree
and helped my sisters, brothers, friends…….

Has shooting stopped? Did Sheku run?
I don't think I can hear.

Apologies all those I hurt
forgive me please I pray………..
it seems to grow much darker -   *why?*
I can't hear you no more……………

"Dust to dust, ashes to ashes"
A sister weeps, a mother wails;
Father and brother stare stonily on
while jubilant troops
plan even deadlier raids.

A SECOND CHANCE?

Lost in thought she sits alone
wondering maybe - what next now?
feed the baby? rivals wound to tend?
or contemplate other beating
from broke teenage spouse faced,
yet again, with his life death choice:
the daily meal or the Premiership?

Sitting by the roadside
tattered laundry in the sun
heaving sighs of deep regret
as old friends skip to school.

Now clear was daddy's warning cry
which she and sisters had ignored
for pretty mother reigned supreme
street cleaner dad best left unknown.

What say you now
little Miss Lay
as beauty fades
and your rival's gain?
Will you holler, will you shout
Will you scream - it's *mummy's* fault?
Or pray and pray that one fine day
A second chance may come your way?

Leoneanthology

Mustapha Sanassie Biro

THE PATRIOT

The patriot seeks not any crusader of jingoism
Nor the camouflage of democracy and nationalism
Finding floor for the flow and flowering of vandalism
This is an outright contravention of patriotism
But he with real and reasonable heart for his land
Whenever the need arises
As he has fully made up his mind
Willingly shall give up existence in defense
Nonetheless you all must rise
All sharing such emotion without pretense
An obligation this should be; not an advice
To evade every union with moral or social decadence

This area of land specified the patriot's fatherland
Ranked with fine plains, rivers and mountains
Its anthem and pledge are worth blowing around
With human and natural resources he'll endeavor to retain,
Live to hail heroines and heroes
Love and respect leaders- not in disguise
And wait to be rewarded by tomorrow
Regardless of whether whimsical is today's price

WAR

The days become squalid:
Jam-packed with melancholy and qualms
The nights rebuff their bosom,
With ascending stars and meteors to kill
Beyond every gut or amend.
The haunted become the hunters
To hoard their precious lives
And tell the uncanny story.

Gbanabom Hallowell

ONE NIGHT AT LUMELY BEACH

I remember one night in a hundred
From the backwaters of an ample Sunday
I ran across the air loving the feel of my sinking feet
In the sandy maize cold at heart befriending my soles.
It is possible to speak of Lumely beach in Atlantic terms,
In terms of an arriving vessel lit in the gloom.
It is possible to speak of this beach in terms of smoke
Oozing from the clouds with star lights seeking
The love of the patient grains.

This waterspout of the lion, from his mountain,
Length to length, the sandy exuberance of the sea
And of the elongation—
One night equals the speed of the chase and the hunger
Of the pack, the human pack in circular advent.
Lovers of the beach Lumely beckons by night and by day.
Here sensation is a climber of trees and of its breeze
Of volume. Splash of the beverage and of the booze,
The sea eats out of the sky lightning by lightning.

Gbanabom Hallowell (ed.)

BUNCE ISLAND ON MY MIND

Island of my instance, healed by your own lugubrious
Syllables bring me closer to the smoke of your embrace.
Cross over my chest for the many slaves that crossed
Over yours. Twisted blood, anchor me beside M.V. Hawkins,
Beside the sadness of its captain's happiness. Within seconds
Of landing, here I am the happiness of the slave, antecedent
Of myself I sing you the shackles of the Negro spirituals.

Assembly of the circular, the famous forgetting
Of those years, the momentary busts of the grey hours—
More than enough Bunce on this Island; the cannon hearts
Their minds, those who built the noisy chains of misery.
The archaic intention, the witnessing birds viewing black
And white the invention of pain, immortal of the mortal;
Island of the servitude I love your courageous centuries.

SOMEONE HAD TO HAVE LOVED MADAM YOKO

Met her against a wall staring at the front wall
Just when the world was coming to an end; sincerely
And theoretically, there had to have been a delighted man
Who decolonized himself under the pressure of this
Universal hate called love; for the sea, when it was
Never an ocean, hummed against stray ships.

This portrait has told a lie. She didn't sit all hour
To stare at a raw wall or at a color peeling
Off its vagaries. In the middle truth, after
The portrait has glided through the white
Face of her majesty's patience it shall then
Be known who it was that loved Madam to death.

THE ECONOMIC MIND OF BAI BUREH

Universal man, his own economic order,
Theory supporting warrior in the
Lynching of the tax man in his dry skin.
Taxing himself, he stood the world on its axis,
The circular thatch fronds polygamous compound
Decoder of the sea under its own theories, and
Of the land under its bottom theory, the fire blazed.

Why it was due another Caesar, this King
Did not know. Why it was him feeding
The mind of the bugler under the effort
Of his own sweat? A Savannah order
Matched with its cyclone, King against Queen.

Night of the conquistador! The black hand
Of betrayal gave Bai Bureh the victory of the truth!
Pink fingers of the cadaver-other wailed in their islands
And in the tender island of his own St. Helena
A wind brought the chorus of the Kasseh coast.

GBANKA OF YONI

He walked up his head into two paths
Down below his navel he was two, two in his sleep
Dreaming a dual duel. His mind was metacarpal, always
Fidgeting the stampede of his sweat. Something met
With him besides himself on the road to Kpa-Mende.

Other matters left him between himself, matters coming
Up against him on the road from Yoni. He swore
By the evening of his name to decide between his duality,
Whether to step his left where his right had stepped out of,
Or to look ahead of his road immediately,
Against the urgent curve.

Between himself he stood with one leg raised. Toward
His pusillanimity a sword broke its demeanor and turned
Into dust of flour; two identities screwed his dour edges.

KAI LONDO OF KAILAHUN

These things when they are said belatedly of Kai Londo
Arrive at the heart with all their unsung passed

He killed another warrior close to the palm of his own hand
And sent off his head to the next pale man

These things when they are written of his sword
The plough of the oracle contends with the eternal silence

Ten hurricanes in his cyclone, the middle passage
Of his Kailahun against the waste of any savannah

Received in the fold of dawn through impossible *pehwabu*[20]
His giant silence went directly for the gargantuan emptiness

---

[20] *Pehwabu: Mende expression for a large open apartment for elderly women in-mates*

I.T.A. WALLACE JOHNSON, COME FORTH

In your peripheral profile a loaf of life comes with its bread
And all other particulars erect themselves a mahogany.
Under, a memorial rail brings your quick wagon alive
Honoring your cargo with a salt of heart; the brimming
Places of your erased footsteps appear on sandy prints
And now your clenched fists O Wallace, in favor
Of the Sierra, tell of your long spoon of hope at dinner,
Colonial of appetite; of the honor of the fists, the feasts,
A daiquiri telling of an African appetite.

O Wallace, you simultaneous countryman, I salute you,
And in the augmentation of your flower for my bread
I kiss your sand that was true to its own mandate; because
Of your simultaneity honor comes to the dinner of the bread,
The liquid of the water, the wind of the breeze, and the man
In our own mortality. Because in your reality the life
Of the sun was longer than that of the day, you were Lazarus
went to sleep in the fertile alcove of a necessary silence.
The dawn is nigh, come forth, therefore, and be huge!

KING KAMA DUMBUYA

King, walking up to your height by the fringes of your name
The nomenclature of the country flattens in its own ball.
In regard to the fjord, the scores of the stars left the field
With you, even in the plantation of your fans, soccer is again
A slave branded in the pain of the imperial fore-chest
Of conscience, and the Leone, together with the only
Dignity of its own Stars has since returned, tear for tear,
To flood the Rokel, weakening its banks and its deposits.
King of the right and of the left leg, standing on dancing,
Your plate of name is absent on the scoreboard as your
Country's capital hazes in the college of the commonwealth.
In the vigil of our stadium we miss you in fields; between
Our eyelids, we no longer know each other as two, you,
Museum of our consolation, we speak truth to you!

A RIVER OF TWO SCARCIES

No longer water in their heavens,
Only the rush of their rivers went through
The weekly purgatory of the Lady's thirst—
In the little greatness of it all, the great littleness, and
A pebble of silence eating serenity by the throat.
Nickel of Caliban returned to Caliban through
The banks and the *Kaba* marshland, also the missing
Scassos sailing to the slavers vastness, the water crying
Through the narrow bone of Kolente
Caliban and the ride, the awkward rush
To wear the insulting crown, the kingship of pain.

Regenerated Caliban in the new waters of the Scarcies,
Sailing the M.V. Miranda in common regalia, serene
On the jackass of the slavers vastness; Gangrene
of the broken nights devoid of African affection; the cyclone
Ends its putrefaction in the middle pole of the sea
Away from the great littleness and the little greatness
Of the twin sisters in the portico of the new canal.
In the influential romance of water and river
The liquid of the fresh drinks against its thirst.
Kilometer by kilometer our ladies of the North,
Side by side, sail Caliban away from the notorious cycle.

AMISTAD OF THE SIERRA

On its own volition, the sea obeyed
The black faith of its pregnancy; where there
Was no Sierra, Spain bled amply under its barometer
Out of that moment came the African occasion
Spain sank away from its Amistad under the foot
Of its flag, it sank at the feet of its perambulation
Amistades Peligrosas
Too much map of freedom delayed Africa on the high seas
In America the conquistador was broken
Because of Sierra Leone
And Africa walked on water in favor of its continent
The bride of the sore throat of Spain
In his futuristic volume Alberto Comesan sang the dirge
The kilometer placard of the American adage
The simple continent of the black eye
The courage of slavery showed in the placard of the slave
And being so tagged, the hour moved its leg
Into the eyes of the brother, the embarrassed sisters
In chains in the middle of a Spanish festival
Where tomorrow's Cristina del Valle was all chorus; there,
where beneath the deck of human spite
A volcano reddened the black skin.

Mohamed Gibril Sesay

WE MARCHON

Pieces of memory
For borderposts

A word
Is bordered by emptiness- on page

Inspeechit`sthememory of speaker/hearer

Thearabs say acquire another language
You acquire another memory

How true how true
We marchon with our un- native accents
Changing wordscapes
Colonising memories
Soyinka is our cortez

In france theAcademy
Reviews residentialpermits
Of alienwords
The Africa poet[21] who helps them
Is our Trojan horse

---

[21] Senghor was a member of the French Academy that certified acceptable French words every year

We marchon
Jonathan swift foresaw this

And cried for an English Academy

This Computer is that dream come true
I wish it Babel's fate for daring to say Sesay
Is really SASSY or SAUCY or…
Back to the programmers
You never learnt my mama tongue

OR FALANG[22]

Or Falang
On any journey to the soul
Karawas[23] cuts on my heart
Salty memories running
Brimstone rumbling
On my being

Or falang
When I'm seeking solace
With another
She becomes her karawas

Fire on me
Fire from the stream
Fire shooting
From the stream

Or falang
Ah kuru[24]
Yes Sokobana[25]

---

[22] Themne belief relating to dead witches and wizards coming back to torment the living
[23] Whip made of hides
[24] Themne name for God
[25] High Officials of Poro, the secret society charged with putting an end to the menace of resurrecting witches and wizards

To the grave
Said the Sokobana

The grave
To the grave
To the time of parting
Ah there she is
As she was
Even more so
Like a shayma fu[26]
Smiling to me
Healing my heart-cuts

No don`t cut[27]
No Sokobana
Into seven places no
No
Spill not that
Un-flowing mystic blood
Defying time
No
I want her whole

---

[26] Woman just out of the initiation ceremony, a paragon of beauty
[27] Reference to how the exhumed corpse is cut into pieces to put an end to the menace

AT THE GATHERING OF THE ROADS

At the gathering of roads
I gather myself within
Like skirts of women
Crossing a stream
This life but a silent scream
Rumbling quick
Like holy mutterings
During Juma[28] Sermon halftime

At the gathering of roads,
I gather myself within,
Like skirts of women pounding rice
Singing Inehtiba
Those joyous confessions of fornication and adultery
To lighten the burden of work

Yea, as our Ramadan advances,
So our scruples
Like the prayer rows at our mosques
Crumble into tempting viands
People-kind is created impatient
Fast-forwarding al fatiha[29]
So as to fight over the sara[30] of ritual murderers.

---

[28] Muslim Friday Congregational prayers
[29] Opening chapter of the Koran, read in almost every Muslim supplications
[30] Offering, charity

As our Ramadan advances,
Weak faith diminishes our congregational numbers

Or, fearing the crowd we baikorkor[31]
Don't be two bellied, the Preachers admonish,
The famished road leads to heaven's gate.

As our Ramadan advances,
My faith, my heart, falls down my stomach
Cannibalistic gastric fluids assail it.
Witches, our people say, eat their own hearts at initiation.
Am I becoming one?

Satanic roaches sulking
In the cracks of walled Ramadan thoughts
But do flies buzz an arse for naught?
Humankind is created weak, from base fluids.
And flies, even fools know, only buzz impurities.

At the gathering of roads
I gather myself within
Like footballers their crotches
On the wall defending a free kick
Few meters from the penalty spot

---

[31] Hiding to eat whilst fasting, but maintaining in public that you are fasting

As our Ramadan advances
The Preacher admonishes
We are also beings of fitra[32]

Essences of the pure breathe
Vultures are nauseated by cleanliness;

The breathing of God within hallows us.
Iblis[33] is envious, would not bow,
God's breath nauseates him

As our Ramadan advances,
I gather myself within,
Like Bilkis[34] her skirt
On stepping on Solomon's glassy floor.

As Our Ramadan advances
The imagination becomes hungrier,
Many travellers have fallen off the Sirati[35] of faith
Into its insatiability

---

[32] In Islam 'state of purity, everybody being born pure, without sin'
[33] In the Koran, another name for Satan
[34] In Koranic exegesis, name for the Queen of Sheba
[35] In Islamic eschatology, bridge over hell that all must pass through on Day of Judgment. Those with faith cross very fast, those with little faith take a while, and those without fall off in to hell

Leoneanthology

But the holy books say we are born to choose
That's the divine right of humans
And born to choose means born to imagine possibilities
Do the woolen ones, the Sufi
Not say there are as many paths to God
As there are human souls
Save that this faith, this new strain, clogs them,
Save one – the straight path,
Submission to the weal of the All Majestic.

Woe then unto poets
Howls the fanatic
Don't you see how their sayings suggest too many
    possibilities?
Don't you see them twist their mouths
To change the sounds of words?
How they wring their lines to confuse straight readers?

O faith, I yearn your certitude, hopeful.
Hoping is dreaming with eyes wide open
To the ultra-violet of Sun-god Ra

Miranda[36] on the Island of the living witch.
That the Father and his Ariels[37] are around

---

[36] In Shakespeare's 'The Tempest,' a young woman almost all alone on an Island

Is an epic lie told by an English poet
To calm the wretchedness of being flung upon yourself
Look, the moralist is the being of the after-here
Stranded on the shores of now.
Maturity, they say, is the downsizing of hope, retrenching dreams.
What do you eat, grace or grass?
Stomach like man who has been gbagba[38]-ed
Rectum knotted by evil ones

Are grass and grace jamsi?[39]
Are purity and impurity mutually exclusive?
Just reflect your being
Is it not made of gore and glow?
Shit and spirit?
Soil and soul?

But what do you glory in
Grass or grace, which do you assert?

---

[37] Reference to Ariel, a goodly spirit in Shakespeare 'The Tempest'
[38] Belief about constipation induced by evil ones, often resulting in death from a swollen belly
[39] A relative, friend or acquaintance, that one is not in speaking terms with now

As our Ramadan advances, hunger eats the insides of our
    vision
The way our people say witches eat the insides of a child
The child is now hollow than an upside down calabash,
Frailer than dangling phlegm
So as our Ramadan advances,
The Preachers conspire to keep our vision steady.
They say: keep vigil, tend your end
Pray the nightly Tahajud[40]
S/he who is awake cannot be bewitched.
At the gathering of roads
I gather myself within
Like tired worshippers their hands
Whilst standing up for the longs verses
Of our Tahajud
Wobbling knees
Tired ankles
Shackled to the holiness
Of the Imam's voice

There were a number of us, remember
At the Bistrot de Paris[41]
When I asked Peter
About the last ten days of his Ramadan.

---

[40] Very long night prayers during the last ten days of Ramadan
[41] Restaurant in downtown Freetown, now closed

Gbanabom Hallowell (ed.)

He said, I'll keep vigil in the cathedrals of England,
Restore the ancient chandeliers,
Put olive oil to fire the wick-glow
Now threatened by the waves of this electricity age.

Sometimes I think their vigil is easier,

It's like a conscience imposed anger at their own kind of
    mess.
Have you ever had a conscience imposed hunger?
They only offer pigs genitals. You wouldn't ch-
Eat, wouldn't baikorkor.
So your belly eats the muscles of your thighs,
Churns your voice wavering like a broadcaster's in an ill-
tuned radio.

You shut your eyes;
You see a delicious plate of angels.
You grab it
You open your eyes.
O, the plate is gone.

Hunger now assails you like frenzy drummers a drum;
The sounds of your hollowness reverberates the world.
O beloved, if the drum is not hollow,
How would the drummers fare?

What would our world dance to?
The piano?
O my Ambiguous Adventures.
Hunger, says Hamidou Kane in his *Ambiguous Adventures*
Is the principal enemy of God (p11, p82).
Pawpaw, our people say, is no benevolent mother
To the inhabitants of the hungry season.

At the gathering of roads
I gather myself within
Like feet of experienced mosque sitters
Soles touching under-thighs
Heels almost butting the under-loins

At the gathering of roads
At the gathering of destinies
At the gathering of possibilities

At the gathering of imaginations
I gather myself within
Like the cupped palms of the fervent hopefuls
Saying Ameen[42]
To the Dua[43] of the Imam

---

[42] Amen
[43] Islamic supplication

And I ask
But what if the hunger is voluntary,
Like in this Ramadan
Would you break your prostrations for koko-ebeh[44]
Would you fast forward the alfatiha
To eat sara of ritual murderers?

O God my God
Grant me will to pray my Tahajud
And may our end be beautiful!

---

[44] Trifle

James Bernard Taylor

DISSIPATING SLOWLY

Through simple contacts
A soul peers at the beauty of another
Pure heartfelt sincerity
With unintentional gaze
Unconsciously creating a yearning for deep commitment
As shadows dance in El Dorado
Lifeless thoughts gain strength
As they feed on the more positive aspirations
Appreciating well savoured responses
Feeding on its buds
And wanting more

Even in its unripe fruitless state
Consumption creates more appetite
To savour the intrinsic qualities
That so appealed to the senses
Venn diagrams interlock
And heartbeats race like grand-prix motors
Feelings heightened
In a cross match of desires
Not deciphering between needs and wants
Slowly
Innocence move into naivety
which moves further into the sublime
Alas
After a while
A Long long while perhaps

       Or
In a twinkling of an eye
Roadblocks appear
And intentions and feelings unsure
Of each other's feelings
Tend to dissipate
In mistrust and rejection
       Yes
Feelings once on the mountain of hope
Will dissipate slowly
Going down from the peak unconsciously climbed
Again unto the soft valley of despair from whence it came

But
It was good to have climbed
And maybe
It will be good to stay halfway up the hill
Neither up nor down
Allowing itself to dissipate slowly

HERE TODAY, GONE TOMORROW
Written in memory of Major Abu Tarawalie who died 24 Feb 1995

One morning
One afternoon
One evening
We entered the universe
Each in his own time
Floating in the air
Not conscious of our being
Ready to accept our role
Whether the script be long or short
    Slowly with time
All became familiar
We saw creatures great and small
Eating, dancing, crying, toiling
Eager to make the day what it should be
Each day brought new happenings
Expected and unexpected
    Moving through the crowd
With my palm branch in my hand
I became like them
Dancing with them
Wailing with them
Eating from my calabash
Drinking from my country pot
    The crowd moved on and on
Swelling and dwindling
Dwindling and swelling
As creatures succumbed to the metamorphoses of life

      Around me
Creatures materialized out of nothing

      And expired into infinity
Some willing
Others unwilling
To leave the crowd behind
      I ran to the stream to cool my head
It was then that I saw him
Tall, handsome and elegant
Waving to me
Trying to say something
      I listened to him and heard a faint farewell
I tried to ask him why he should expire so soon
I tried to plead with him to stay
      Yes
I saw the unwillingness to depart in those cool eyes
I also saw the helplessness
As he tried to placate the gods to allow him to stay
      He stretched forth his hand
And I reached out to bring him out of the water
But I touched shadows
      Yes
Shadows that disappeared through my fingers
      He sank beneath the waves
His fingers thrashing the water
Until the last ripple died with him

    Disappointed
I turned around
weeping in my innocence

    The crowd moved on
Weary skeletals left behind
Moved on and on
Trying to catch the attention of the gods
To hasten their expiration
To go down the water in his stead

    But
They were left against their will
As the crowd repeated the cycle of life
    I stood for a moment
And looked around at the crowd
The righteous
The wicked
The saint
The devil
All mingling in their sweat
    I looked at the spot
Where I saw the last ripple in the stream
Hoping to see my friend come up one last time
    He sank so fast
The stream was now calm again

I smiled bitterly
And I wondered….
Who will be next

I REFUSE!

I refuse to be unnatural to myself
I refuse to be untrue to my conscience
I refuse to wear borrowed garments
I refuse to be molested
I refuse to be blindfolded
I refuse to be spoon-fed
I refuse to go on an empty stomach amidst plenty
I refuse to live in squalor
I refuse to eat refuse
I refuse to be struck by lightning from man-made gods
I refuse to go barefooted on pricks and stones
I refuse to be told what is not good for me
I refuse to not have my dignity
I refuse to be dirty while at the river
I refuse to be skeletal and hungry at the feast
I refuse to not have what I deserve
I refuse!
I refuse!
I refuse!
In my Serra Lyoa
The land of milk and honey.

Leoneanthology

Ambrose Massaquoi

SLEEPLESS IN AMERICA

I dreamt sleep in the USA
To perch on the roadside
Where the blaze of Sundance
Has not consumed the corn

On the roadside
In the corn
The scheme of Sun
Is dance of sickle
In my eyes

Moon…Moon
That immemorial
Sycophant of Sun is
Fishhook in the flesh
Of my sleep

Sun jerks the hook
Sickle slashes skin
Down my spine
Tears sleep
From my dream

And I am forced to backslide
To tears

Back into the blaze of Sundance

Leoneanthology

IBADAN REVISTED

With its own reckless hands
This conurbation has completely wrecked itself
The far-flung roofs of its slums rot with rust in bloodsucking
Sun
Along cracked skulls of its carriageways, traffic is dead...
Festers beside carcasses of cars, trucks, trailers, tankers,
tippers, *okadas*
Killed by cutthroat mechanics
Only cacophony survives the collateral scrapping
Even Clark's glimmering seven hills have died under this
crushing
Spread of man

EPITAPH

For my son who died at birth

Your face
From the long distance
Of elephant's memory

Your face
Lazarus come forth
Smack out of my loins

Fair-skinned sesame
Seeds of your face
More fertile than death

Face with footprints—
As pregnant turtle's—
Beamed from beyond stars

Always lights a child's first
Smile of solace on my
Father face

COUNTERPOINT

In memory of Uncle Ben-1 Cor. 15:54

You have fired a first finger
Into the eye balls of death
And have burned down the shiver
In the cold hold of its shadow and stare

So the old man
           The grave
                     With his boat
Full of his own ashes
            Floats
   Adrift
                Towards the edge
Where his infernal river falls off to drown in
Abyss

You have packed lavish laughter
Into life's lip-lock with loss
Romanced a widow's drawn out dirge
To jazz and dance on the wingspan of Seraphs

Let now the low
              Doleful drum
Beat of saints
              Shuffle & swing
      Lift a lilt

While you
Waltz a-
Cross rhythms to enter eternal supernal
Bliss

GRASSROOTS POET
To Gbanabom Hallowell, for gathering us into FPS

I am Falui
One-armed combustive poet
Twin brother of Elephant Grass

I who once stabbed my
Heart with torments for my Sierra
Shattered my grit on her
Peaks of pain

I now by the spirit of grassroots
Dance with bushfire &
Carry fury in memory of
Cobra smoked out of his hold

I uncoil my fangs into vibes
On the fire of all Sierra's rivers
To become a sea of poets
Skilled in rising from death

And I arise… I rise
Through the taproot tip of Cotton Tree
I emerge to surge through Sierra's bones
To purge forever from the marrows of memory

The scandal of rapscallions
Turgid in the conch of
Her pubescence

Miatta French

OFFERING TIME

I beg to differ from your religion Sire.
It doesn't look good from where I'm sitting.
I beg to differ - Even though I like the sound of your choir
I think there's a bit more that I would require.
What gives you the right
To demand my mother's widow's mite
So she can't cook for us tonight?
Because you must preach from a bigger space?
I beg to differ Sire!

TO SISTERS IN HIGH PLACES

Let the Sisters know that we are rooting for them!
Yes, tell them we appreciate them.
That now that they have reached the top
They cannot stop
They must continue to insist,
Persist and struggle not desist,
For the sake of those who barely exist.
Let the Sisters know…

CONTRACT FOR PREGNANCY

It would be good to have you rub my back
Through waves of morning sickness.
It would great to know you understand
That being tired isn't a weakness.
And when my prenatal visits run late
To be assured that you would wait.
Yes, put your arms around my waist
And not revile its thickness.

IT'S NEVER RIGHT WHEN MAMA GOES

Mama! I don't know you.
You left; there was nothing I could do.
I can't miss what I never had?
Forget it! Nothing can be this bad.
For you it was all pain no gain.
For me a life of stress and strain.

Mama, I knew you well.
So many stories I have to tell.
I've had you long, I'm glad you're gone?
No never! Your work can't have been done.
Oh yes indeed you stayed the course.
For this I fear I'm all the worse.

Gbanabom Hallowell (ed.)

Kosonike Koso-Thomas

FISHWOMAN

I sell fish at Krootown Road market,
Like all who trade in the same kind of goods;
Raw fish, dried fish, whole fish or prime cuts,
Any fish which sells is good business for me.
I wake up at dawn and scout the wharves
For the catch of the morning or the night before,
Then off to the market to make a block[45] or two
I'm approached by women looking for bargains.
They have left their husbands snug in bed
Who must sit to breakfast when they're back;
But I have my man still combing the sea
To land a net full of fish for skulks like them.
One woman looks up and asks me my price
For a gruppa of average size.
She's dressed in blue; headtie to match,
There's good money in her handbag I reckon.
So I charge her the earth, ten thousand a cut
She hisses and growls back, "too much"
I eye her with fury, she looks away.
She has millions in her bag but shields them.
" I pay two thousand and that's all," she shouts.
Then mumbles, "You people think money grows on trees."
I want to scratch her eyes, her powdered face, and all
But said instead, "go fish with your husband in bed."

---

[45] Block: colloquial term for Le100.

THE PEN ROAD

I've walked over many a rugged hill
This ancient road to map
Instruments in hand, limbs in deep peril
I paced through every mishap.

Years past this road was much fun to drive
From Lumley in the west end
To Waterloo in the urban divide.
Then paved, day trips were the trend.

Just off its northerly edge waves beat
On silvery beaches serene;
Trees line both sides, their branches bend to greet
The deeply fractured earth between.

The narrow passage left for me to tread
I share with dump trucks a speeding,
Their exhaust fumes and dust from the roadbed,
Leave my weakening lungs chocking.

There's a stretch from Freetown to Tokeh
In state car owners most fear
Potholed and ridged its pavement's a wreck
That rips tyres front and rear.

The road leads to beach sites with every thrill
But none walks it who needs not

Subject arms and legs to a dancing drill
Round boulders, like a robot.

Villagers complain the road's poor state
Bars visits to choice resorts;
Yet beach lovers in increasing rate
Risk all for love of sea sports

Throughout its length, the Pen road snakes through
Wide plains and many a river catchment
Which stay dry as bones till the rains fall due
And feed their pores absorbent.

Then torrents of rain water flood the streams
Rising in menace of bridges frail
To overtop decks and soffit beams
And wash down the odd handrail.

'Tis known these bridges seat astride time
That antiquates each site.
They have a tale to tell of lives prime
Lost in those crossings at night

Tomb stones at Comfort and John Obey
Mark sites of driving errors.
There kinsfolk oft stop to mourn, as they

Remember dead ancestors.
I recall setting survey stations
With painted pins drilled in wood blocks.
I sight a line clear of obstructions
Above ground strewn with sharp rocks

As I pace the line to fix a peg
I slip on a hard rock face
The torque on the ankle of my leg
Force that joint out of place.

My boot straps in place provide a brace
But I stay still as seems best.
The pain is growing, my pulses race
I yell a curse in protest.

I'm forced to quit with little to plot
As base for design, yet feel no guilt
When crowds round me ask what news I've got
Of this road being ever built.

WASHER WOMAN

She moves through the fields,
A load of washing on her head
The child on her back nests its head
On the deep of her spine,
And sleeps as dew drops fall.

She had been to the brook
Where the village folks wash
All manner of dirty clothes;
And had soaked and soaped
And rubbed and beat, till dark.

Whites, garas, wax printed lappas;
Gowns from father, mother and kids.
She'd pounded and threshed like rice stalks,
High and low on waterside stones,
Till dirt from the pile oozed out.

Then with hands bleached and bruised
By the soda in the soap,
She had rinsed them all in the pool
'Neath the flowing sparkling brook,
And squeezed and wringed till dry.

She thinks now of the house she must clean
The food to cook when her man gets back
From the fields where he earns a wage
Not enough to pay the rent

But harvests unseen to make him more.
He pictures his wife nearing home with hope
And a plan for the evening meal.
He worries a bit that the loot from the fields
May not fit the plan she has made,
And wonders how is wife will react.

What a life he thought he now lives
That hangs on a thin bread line,
Propped by hands that cheat and trick?
He'll reach home confused
To face wife and child in disgust.

He will blame the world
For the state of his life,
His country, for jobs he can't have
He'll swear his bosses will sing in hell
For paying him less than he's due.

Frederick Borbor James

THE JOURNEY

In a stupor he arrived in this place
Receiving close attention
Three golden years he was a king
Everyone his kind attendant
The first golden year a keen observer
Asking varied questions
His chief attendant a genius
Decoding his every babble

Emerging from his ecstasy
He found himself on a journey
Back to where he had soporifically come from
Life is a journey
To an unknown destination
On a thorny rugged smooth path
Some go at fast pace
Others at a snail's pace
To this an unknown destination

So here he goes on this journey
With a host of others
Yet going alone
Never choosing to be on this journey
But at his maker's behest h journeys
Expected to give account on arrival

THE GAME OF CHIMPS

It was only yesterday
You set loose the dogs
And chased the chimps away
To save our forest from degradation
You say the chimps have big mouths
Which they cram with the meager resources of our forest
Rough fingers with which they ravage our beautiful flowers
But today - just today
You begin to fill to bursting point
Your tiny mouths
With even the little that is left
Of our troubled resources
And crush our fragile flowers
Between your patriotic fingers
Now tell me
Why for heaven's sake
Did you hound the chimps away

FAINT HOPE

Let me stretch out my ailing hands
And feel the fragile peace
Rippling across my reeking land
Let me fill my lungs
With this air of peace
And cleanse my entrails
Ruptured by hopelessness
Caused by untold carnage

Let me take off my clothes
And bathe in this river of peace
It will bring back
My amputated limbs
My gouged out eyes
And ears that have been severed

Oh let me drink this river of peace
It will fertilize my womb
And I'll reproduce en mass
To replenish the thousands
Who were felled by bullets
Machetes and prolonged hunger

Let the rain of peace
Patter upon this land
To expiate the sins
Of wanton killing rape and torture

And precipitate unity and growth
Let me take a walk
In this shadow of peace
And not fall into an ambush
Step on land mine or walk into a booboo trap
Now let me go back home
And live the remnant of my life
In peace and not in pieces

ODE TO TOM CAUURAY

The sun will rise tomorrow
And the muse will come knocking at his door
Rise up and take your pen
You have an unfinished story to write
The sun will set tomorrow and darkness will creep in
Then the muse will come quietly whispering to him
Don't burn your candle at both ends
Put your pen down and go to sleep
The story you are spinning is long and for posterity
The sun rises again tomorrow, darkness falls
And suddenly there is a void
Images grow tall, moving in different directions
The muse comes again to the committed storyteller
I have come several times now
But where are you
For some time I have not heard your forceful voice that cuts through the air
I have not heard your giant gaits that pound the ground
Don't sleep too long
Everyone is waiting for that story to unfold
No matter how long it takes to tell
The storyteller's pen is lying idle in the dust
He is taking a long rest
I can see his giant footprints boldly imprinted on the stage

Leoneanthology

And hear his lyrics rippling across the nation—
Across the world
He has departed from the stage
But his footsteps continue to reverberate in the air

CONTRIBUTORS

Agyeman Taqi is an information and communications technology consultant. He lives in Freetown with his wife and their three children. He is passionate about sports development and is also a licensed coach for the English Football Association.

Ambrose Massaquoi was born in Tongo Fields, Eastern Sierra Leone. He received his education in Christ the King College and Fourah Bay College. He has been a member of the Sierra Leone Association of Writers and Illustrators (SLAWI), Falui Poetry Society, and the newly established Sierra Leone Writers Guild. He is also an Honorary Fellow of writing of the University of Iowa in the USA, where he participated in the International Writing Program in 1994. His poems and short stories have appeared in Sierra Leonean and international publications. He presently lives with his family in Lagos, Nigeria.

Arthur Edgar Smith was born and schooled in Freetown, Sierra Leone. He has been teaching English since 1977 at the Prince of Wales School and Milton Margai College of Education. He is now at Fourah Bay College where he has been lecturing English, Literature, as well as Creative Writing for the past seven years rising to the rank of Senior Lecturer. Mr. Smith is widely published with his writings appearing in local newspapers as well as in *West Africa Magazine*, *Index on Censorship*, *Focus on Library and Information Work*, *Suite101*, *shvoong.com* amongst others. He was one of 17 international visitors who participated in a seminar on contemporary

American Literature in the US from June to August 2006. His growing thoughts and reflections on this trip which took him to various US sights and sounds in Louisville, San Francisco, Cincinnati and Washington D.C. could be read at http://www.lisnews.org. His other publications include *Folktales from Freetown*.

Delphine King was the second Sierra Leonean woman to ever publish a book length volume of poetry after Gladys Casely-Hayford. *Twilight of Dreams* was published in 1968 in Nigeria where the poet had made a name for herself in journalism and the arts. The foreword to her collection was written by Chinua Achebe. King now lives in London, The U.K. She is in her 80s, and still has a passion for poetry.

Elizabeth L. A. Kamara grew up in the east end of Freetown and attended the Annie Walsh Memorial School. She has a B.A. (Hons.) degree in English Language and Literature and a Master of Arts degree, both from the University of Sierra Leone. She currently lectures Literature in English in the Department of Language Studies, Fourah Bay College. She is married with two sons.

Fatou Wurie is a communications and branding strategist who considers herself a storyteller. Fatou holds a BA in political science and gender studies from the University of British Columbia (UBC). She hails from a strong communications background acting as CEO and managing director at Free{the}Town, a communications and branding firm that specializes in African grown projects, brands and campaigns with clients like UNICEF, Health Poverty Action

(HPA), AFFORD SL, Sweet Salone and Sierra Leone National Shipping Carrier (SLNC), EcoMed, to name a few. Fatou is a TEDx Freetown organizer, columnist at *Standard Times Newspaper* and a blogger for the *Huffington Post*. Fatou has been featured on *AfroElle magazine* and joined famed poets from around Africa at the StoryMoja Literary Feastival in Kenya. Fatou believes in stories and their ability to gestate creativity and generate innovation and change for a future where anything is possible.

Fatou Taqi, née Cole was born in Freetown. She holds a PhD in English and currently lectures at Fourah Bay College, University of Sierra Leone. She is a wife and a mother; she enjoys travelling and networking. Her interest areas are in women's and children's development.

Frederick Bobor James was born December 23, 1954 at Yinnie village in Ngawo chiefdom, Bo district. He obtained primary and secondary education in Bumpe, his chiefdom headquarters; and tertiary education in Freetown. Frederick is a teacher, adult educator and development communicator. He is currently a Communication for Development Specialist at UNICEF Sierra Leone Country Office.

Gbanabom Hallowell is the author of *Manscape in the Sierra: New & Collected Poems: 1991-2011* and editor of *In the Belly of the Lion: An Anthology of New Sierra Leonean Short Stories*. His novel, *The Road to Kaibara* was published by SLWS in 2015. Hallowell holds a PhD in Interdisciplinary Studies in the Social Sciences from The Union Institute & University, Ohio, USA, an MFA in Creative Writing and Literature from

Vermont College, USA, an Executive Education in Global Leadership & Public Policy in the 21st Century from the School of Kennedy, Harvard University, Cambridge, USA and a Higher Teachers Certificate from the then Milton Margai Teachers College, Sierra Leone. He has taught at universities both in the United States and in Sierra Leone. He is the Director-General of the Sierra Leone Broadcasting Corporation (SLBC). A 2006 recipient of the Young Global Leadership Award from the World Economic Forum, Hallowell is a member of the Poro Society Sierra Leone (MPSSL).

Isa Espadon Blyden was born in Boston, Massachusetts in the U.S.A in 1951. She has said that her mother was the earliest writer she ever met and Christopher Okigbo the first poet she met. Okigbo persisted in calling her his "wife" and in predicting that she would be a poetess when she was ten years old. At that tender age she also encountered Vincent Chukwuemeka Ike who was a neighbour. When he published his book *Toads for Supper* it was a major event, for Blyden's mother had edited the manuscript. Since then she has been writing mostly prose where she feels most comfortable, though poetry seems to come without her bidding. She says she enjoys the imagery and daring thoughts that they come with. She has had poems published in several journals including "Sekou Toure Dies", in *West Africa Magazine*, "A Myth", "Tekrur", "Ndakaru", "Aline Sitoye Diatta" in *This Month in Dakar*. She is currently a film maker, writer, audio book producer and novelist in progress. Blyden currently lives in Sierra Leone, but has also resided in Liberia, Senegal and Russia. She describes herself as a West African-

American who enjoys the rich, strong erudite and eclectic heritage left her by her great grand-parents—writers, teachers, travelers and innovators. She hopes to bring out her novels in 2014, and she believes that God will be the most relieved to learn of them!

James Bernard Taylor presently serves the US Embassy in Freetown as Director, Information Resource Center. Prior to that he taught at the Methodist Girls High School and at the Institute of Public Administration and Management (IPAM), University of Sierra Leone (Social Work Program). He is a published writer and poet with some of his works found in *Songs That Pour the Heart: Poems from Sierra Leone* and *The Price and Other Stories*. He has also written many non-fictional pieces on socio-political issues in several newspapers. Taylor also plays some musical instruments, including the Piano/Organ and Euphonium and has a passion for classical music and jazz.

Josephine M. Ansumana was a Fulbright Fellow at Rutgers University, New Jersey. She holds a Master's in Business Administration (MBA) and a Master's in Human Resource Management from Marymount University in Arlington, Virginia, USA. She is the author of the collection, *Poems of a Shattered Heart* published by Author House in 2008, in the USA. She has had poems in two American anthologies, on-line magazines, and the Sierra Leone local print media. Ansumana is actively engaged in exploring other creative outlets. She is an Executive Member and Treasurer of the newly launched Sierra Leone Writers Guild. She lives in Freetown, Sierra Leone, and currently works as a Financial

Analyst at the National Commission for Privatization.

Karamoh Kabba is a Sierra Leonean writer, politician and activist. Mr. Kabba is the author of *A Mother's Saga, Lion Mountain* and *Marquee*. He is also a social commentator and political analyst. Many of his short stories, perspectives and analyses on social and political issues have been published in renowned international literary magazines, anthologies and major news outlets worldwide. Mr. Kabba joined the Government of Sierra Leone in 2008 as National Coordinator of the Open Government Initiative (OGI) in the Ministry of Presidential and Public Affairs. He was appointed Director of Political and Public Affairs in the Ministry of Political and Public Affairs, and later Deputy Minister.

Komba David Sandi was born at Jaiama in the Kono District. He holds a B.A. Honours Degree in English from Fourah Bay College, University of Sierra Leone. Proprietor, Ahkom Secondary School, and Ahkom Technical Vocation, Kono, Sandi holds an M.A in Peace and Development Studies, Njala University. He has contributed to and edited several local newspapers. Sandi has been a professional teacher and businessman since his undergraduate studies.

Kosonike Koso-Thomas is an engineer, artist, and poet. He has published several technical articles, two biographies, two books on university development in Sierra Leone and a book of poems. Some of his paintings have been exhibited in Sierra Leone, Nigeria and the United Kingdom. He was a former Vice Chancellor of the University of Sierra Leone,

Fulbright Professor and Research Engineer at the University of California, Berkeley, and visiting scholar at the University of Cambridge. He is currently Chairman of the Tertiary Education Commission of Sierra Leone.

Miatta French is currently one of the five members of the National Electoral Commission (NEC) of Sierra Leone. She has previously served the Commission as head of its Outreach and External Relations Unit and as Director of Operations. She has always been very interested in the performing arts and entertainment generally and has participated in various live theatre and recorded performances. Her major passion has always been for words as she believes that words must be measured like the ingredients of a dish so that meanings come out as they are really meant to be said. "It is important to say what you mean, because meaning what you say can be compromised by your actions," she believes.

Mohamed Gibril Sesay grew up in Crojimmy, Eastern Freetown. He was educated at Fourah Bay College, University of Sierra Leone. His creative work include a novel, *This Side of Nothingness*, a Caine Prize nominated short story, "Halfman and the Curse of the Ancient Buttocks" included in the anthology *"Work in Progress and Other Stories"* Published by Caine Prize (2009). Another short story, "Monkey Teeth" was published in *Focus on Africa Magazine* October-December, 1999. Sesay has had several of his poems published in local and international publications. He has worked as a Sociology lecturer, a journalist and a consultant for various national and international organizations.

Moses Kainwo studied in Sierra Leone. He is married with two daughters and enjoys taking his family out to dinner. He used to see writing as a reasonable pastime for quite some time. Of late, he is beginning to enjoy the exercise and sees no harm in trying his talent with various genres of literature. He uses his writing to also pass on moral statements that highlight some of the anomalies of society.

Mustapha Sanassie Biro was born in Kukuna, Bramaia Chiefdom, Kambia District in 1985. He is twelfth in the row of thirteen children. He attended the Islamic Primary and Secondary Schools in koidu Town, kono District, Kambia District Education Committee (KDEC) Primary School in Kukuna, and the Ahmadiyya Muslim Secondary School in Freetown before graduating Fourah Bay College, University of Sierra Leone with a Bachelor of Arts General in Linguistics and a Diploma in Cultural Studies in 2010. Biro has served as columnist for various newspapers, and sub-Editor for *The Financial Times*, and the *Examiner Newspaper*, both in Freetown. He was English Language Instructor at Rick's institute, Monrovia, Liberia, and Registrar, Snap-Tech Institute in Freetown. He is currently the casting Director, Mercy Movies Production (MMP), and the Editor of the *Daily Express*. He aspires to be an accomplished poet, novelist, musician, actor, script writer, and civil society activist.

P. M. Wilson is a Sierra Leonean writer. He has written numerous stories and plays that are said to transcend the common African allegory. He writes in French and English. Playwright and poet, Wilson is the author of the drama, *Holy Sin*. He took a B.Sc. Honours degree in B.I.T from Njala University. Wilson has also written children's books that have been highly recommended for supplementary school use, by authorities of the Ministry of Education in Sierra Leone.

Prince E. A. J. Kenny was born in Freetown. He attended the Prince of Wales Secondary School and the Methodist Boys' High School. He holds an HTC from Milton Margai College of Education in French, English and Education, a Bachelor of Arts in French Linguistics and Literature and a Master of Arts degree in French Linguistics and Literature from Gamel Abdel Nasser University, Conakry, Guinea, a Master of Science in Sociology, and a Master in Education, University of Sierra Leone. He is currently Senior Lecturer in French and Head of Language Studies Department at Fourah Bay College, University of Sierra Leone. Among the short plays he has published are "Joe Lemoh the Great", "Disappointed", "Life is Pleasant", "Caught", and "La Solution"

Richmond Smith was born in Freetown, and was educated there and in the United Kingdom, Bradford College and Leeds, Metropolitan University, where he took a BSc. (Hons.) degree. He recently returned to Sierra Leone and briefly worked for the Ministry of Tourism, representing his community as a cultural ambassador. Currently, he describes himself as self-employed and has set-up an organization that aims to promote "Getto" communities in urban areas. He is working on his first collection of poems titled *Black*

Richmond. He describes himself as a Quaker, a Pan-Africanist, a social commentator and a live musician.

Siaka Kroma was born in Sierra Leone. He holds a PhD in Education with specialization in Curriculum Theory from the University of Toronto. He began his education at the St. Andrew's Secondary School, the Bo Government Secondary School, and the Albert Academy. He was a pioneer student at Njala University College. He also holds a BA (Ed) degree in English and Education from the University of Sierra Leone and an MLitt in Linguistics from Edinburgh University. He has taught in secondary schools and universities in Sierra Leone and the United States of America. He is retired and lives in Kenya. He visits Sierra Leone regularly. He is the author of the Gomna series of novels: *Gomna's Children, A Corner of Time,* and *Climbing Lilies.*

Talabi Aisie Lucan a distinguished Sierra Leonean educationist, educator and activist was born in 1921. She was educated in Sierra Leone, the United Kingdom and in the United States. She graduated with a Bachelor of Arts degree in History, French and Sociology from Ohio State University in 1961 and a post-graduate diploma in Curriculum and Book Development from Indiana University in 1962. She has since launched a systematic and extensive textbook publishing, mainly for children. Several decades into her career, the University of Sierra Leone awarded her, *Honoris Causa*, Doctor of Letters, for her extensive and authoritative publications in the creative arts, history and social sciences. A popular read in the Sierra Leonean school system, Lucan is also the author of a seminal biography, *The*

Life and Times of Paramount Chief Madam Ella Koblo Gulama. At age 92, Dr. Lucan gladly responded to my request, and submitted three short stories for this anthology. One can only conclude that fresh new manuscripts still continue to roll from this indefatigable talent.

Oumar Farouk Sesay, born in 1960, was resident playwright of Bai Bureh Theatre in the '80s. He studied Political Science and Philosophy at Fourah Bay College, University of Sierra Leone. He has written several plays and served as a columnist for several newspapers. He has been published in many anthologies of Sierra Leonean writers and poets, including *Lice in the Lion's Mane, Songs That Pour the Heart, Kalashnikov In the Sun* and recently *The Price and Other Stories*. His first volume of poems, *Salute to the Remains of a Peasant* was published in 2007 in America. He was Cadbury Visiting Fellow in 2009 at the Center for West African Studies in Birmingham. He is currently working in the private sector as General Manager of his own company. Sesay has noted that his poetry is influenced by poets like John Keats, Thomas Gray, Pablo Neruda, Wole Soyinka and his Sierra Leonean fellow poet, Syl Cheney-Coker.

Printed in the United States
By Bookmasters